FIREFIGHTER INTERVIEW RULE BOOK

SECOND EDITION

MIKE ZOLIN
· AND
ROB CHRISTENSEN

Published By TopScore
Interview911.com Publications

Copyright © 2018 All rights reserved. No part of this book or site may be reproduced or redistributed in any form or by any electronic or mechanical means, including information storage and retrieval systems, without permission from Z Innovations LLC, or DBA TopScore.

Disclaimer: The author(s), publisher, and distributors particularly disclaim any liability, loss, or risk taken by individuals who directly or indirectly act on information contained herein. All readers must accept full responsibility for their use of this material. The information in this book is the work and opinion of the authors and does not represent official opinions or practices of their respective departments, organizations, and associations or any others.

Thanks to our editors: Stefan De Vries, Kelly Cope, Hannah Rhinehart, Jessica Lindley, Erika Neldner

Book Cover Design by www.ebooklaunch.com

This book is brought to you by TopScore and www.interview911.com

This book is dedicated to two people. First, to you, the reader, for committing to starting your career in the fire service off right and giving the interview process everything you have. Keep that level of dedication throughout your career.

Second, this book is dedicated to those who have already trusted us with teaching them how to dominate their interview. These clients (our TopScore family) put in the work and prepared as if their dream career was dependent on it. Furthermore, they've referred friends and family and provided feedback of their experience and ideas, which helped make the second edition possible. Thank you for trusting in us and believing in our product for the most important interview of your life.

"I was told a member of the interview board said, 'In all my years of sitting on these interview panels, that is the first time a candidate walked out of the room and I knew that was our guy.'"

Fritz Gibson

"Mike Zolin and Rob Christensen, I am writing today to let both of you know that the information and instruction that you gave is second to none. I have been offered positions with two different Fire Departments as a direct result of the high interview scores that I received."

R. Pettinger
Valedictorian F.D.N.Y Spring 2002 Recruit Class

"My very first testing experience was with the largest department in the state. I somehow got lucky and passed the written test all on my own, so I decided I would prepare for the oral board on my own, too. Big mistake! I was clueless of how the oral board process works, and needless to say, I did not get the job. Two years later, the same department was testing again so I decided to get some help, and I'm so glad I did. After working with the guys at TopScore, my oral board score skyrocketed from an 80 to a 95! The second time around I DID get the job, and now I'm working for my dream department. I know I would not be a firefighter here today if it weren't for TopScore!"

B. Skovlin

"With the help of their Firefighter Interview Rule Book and Workbook, I received a 100 percent on my interview and a job offer. The first time I tested for this department I was underprepared and overwhelmed. Needless to say, the interview did not go well. My friend told me about the book and the TopScore program. I read Firefighter Interview Rule Book twice, completed the Workbook and met with Rob for interview coaching."

Matthew

Table of Contents

Preface 1

Introduction 5

Chapter 1 Getting Started 9
    A: The Application Process 9
    B: Written Test 10
    C: Physical Aptitude Test 10

Chapter 2 Oral Interview Preparation 13
    A: Interview Overview 13
    B: Interview Preparation 14
    C: Learn the Job Description 15
    D: Your First Impression 18
    E: Second Impression 19
    F: Dress for Success 20
    G: Question Types 20

Chapter 3 TopScore Top5 System 23
    A: TopScore Top5 Overview 23
    B. TopScore Top5 Components 26

Chapter 4 Real Questions and Example Answers 37
    A: Real Question Example 1 37
    B: Real Question Example 2 39
    C. Real Questions Example 3 41

Chapter 5 The "What If" Interview Questions 45
    A: The "What If" Questions Overview 45
    B: Leading Questions 46
    C: Situational Questions 49
    D: Interpersonal Questions 53
    E: Bizarre, Weird, or Just Different Questions 54

Chapter 6 Core Values, Skills, and Abilities **57**
   A: Overview: Core Values 57
   B: Skill and Abilities 58

Chapter 7 Marketing Priorities **69**
   A: TopScore Marketing Priorities 69
   B: Example Marketing Priorities 70
   C: Marketing Priorities Blended into TopScore 72

Chapter 8 Oral Interview Wrap Up **75**
   A: Closing Remarks 75
   B: Thank You Card 76
   C: Additional TopScore Rules for the Oral Interview 76
   D: Sample Questions 79
   E: Example "What If" Questions 83

Chapter 9 Ride-along Rules **85**
   A. About the Ride-along 85
   B: Ride-along Rules 85
   C. Ride-along Questions 87

Chapter 10 Mock Interviews and Self Score Rubrics **89**
   A: An Overview to Practice 89
   B: Filling in Your Own Scoresheet 90
   C: TopScore Interview Scoresheet 91
   D: TopScore Top5 Scorecard 93

Chapter 11 Preparation Timeline **97**
   A: Preparation Timeline 97
   B: Congratulations! 100

About the Authors **101**

Preface

(*see Figure 1 for Diagram)

There is a lot of information in this book; we will start with a brief summary of the fundamental concepts. Just keep them in mind; we will cover them in full detail later in the book.

There are two types of interview questions: Real and What If.

1. Real Questions: These interview questions are exactly what they sound like. They are about you and your life experiences. You will learn how to answer Real Questions using the TopScore Top5. This is where you blend five parts to make one complete answer.
2. What If Questions: These questions are hypothetical. There are three types of What If Questions.
    a. Situational
    b. Leading
    c. Interpersonal

The TopScore system consists of the following parts:

1. TopScore Top5: A framework to help provide structure to your answers of the Real Questions portion of the firefighter interview.
2. Core Values: The guiding principles that dictate your behavior and actions. Core Values are blended with the TopScore Top5 during the Oral Interview process.
3. Marketing Priorities: The highlights from your life. Marketing Priorities are the things you want the oral board to know about you. Some, but not all, of these priorities can be gathered from your résumé. Your Marketing Priorities are communicated during your Oral Interview by blending them with the TopScore Top5.

4. Rules: During a Fire Department interview, there are many important things you need to do and say. Probably more importantly, however, are things you should not do or say. These important pieces of information are what we like to call The Rules. You'll learn over 60 rules to guide your interview process.

For additional interview support and preparation see the Firefighter Interview Rule Book Workbook and Interview911.com for personalized interview coaching.

fig. 1: Visual Overview of Summary Section

Visual Overview: Fundamental Concepts

TopScore Answers

TopScore Top5
This five-part system is designed to allow candidates to construct dynamic and winning answers during the Real Questions portion of interview through the following components:
1) Answer the Question
2) Personal History (PH)
3) Personal Story (PS)
4) Department Knowledge (DK)
5) Keywords (KW)

Marketing Priorities
Marketing Priorities are your personal highlights that communicate your positive attributes, skills, and potential to an organization. Blend with the TopScore Top5 in the oral interview.

Core Values
Core Values are your fundamental beliefs and guiding principles that dictate your behavior and actions. Blend with the TopScore Top5 in the oral interview.

The Rules
The Rules govern all parts of the interview process. This includes the application process, actual interview, and the interview follow-up. Many of these rules are unspoken, yet often are the difference between securing a position or continuing the job hunt. You'll learn over 70 of these rules.

Introduction

(see Figure 2 for Diagram)

Attaining a position as a professional firefighter is considered by many to be impossible. It is not uncommon to hear a Fire Department having 2,000 applicants for no more than 20 available positions. Quick math will tell you your initial odds could be as low as 1 percent. With these odds, it is clear why so many people call it impossible. It is our goal as coaches to make it POSSIBLE!

This book will not give you answers to 101 different interview questions. If we answered all of the questions for you, the answers would be ours, not yours. Instead, you'll get the tools to answer any question with a simple-to-understand, five-step process.

The oral board doesn't give a perfect score lightly; they look for very specific details. Once you know these details, they will improve your score dramatically.

There are four major components in this book. They include the TopScore Top5, the TopScore Marketing Priorities, Core Values, and The Rules.

TopScore Top5 is the foundation for answering questions and the TopScore Marketing Priorities are the polish to ensure you've not only answered the question, but that you also have provided the oral board with enough information to really understand who you are and what you are capable of.

Core Values are your fundamental beliefs and guiding principles that dictate your behavior and actions that must be communicated to the oral board. We will teach you how to blend Core Values and Marketing Priorities with the TopScore Top5 in order to construct and articulate winning answers!

Think of the hiring process as a competition, designed to separate the good from the best. However, as with any competition, there are rules.

You must learn The Rules before your first interview. You will see that parts of the interview are like playing a game, and knowing The Rules will help you be victorious in this game.

The final key element to being victorious is having a great team. This is where the TopScore team comes in. Over the last 15 years, our team of successful candidates continues to grow. We are glad you picked us as part of your team. We have been down the path to victory and played the game many times.

While this book has all the information you need to nail your interview, some interviews may differ from the average interview. There is no way for us to know the details about every interview you could encounter, so do your research before you start the process.

We understand the time and expense that is involved in testing to become a firefighter. Our goal is to help you cut down the amount of time, energy, and expense involved in your pursuit of this amazing career. Our only caveat to your purchase of this book is the following: be dedicated to attaining your career, and when you are hired, remain passionate for this great profession!

To truly grasp and implement the concepts discussed in this book, you will need to practice, and when you feel you have mastered the TopScore system, practice some more! Yes, this takes effort—a lot of effort—but keep your goal in sight. If you need some motivation, find out when your local fire academy is holding a graduation and attend. You'll probably feel a little queasy as you watch the badges being pinned on the newest firefighters. Refocus that envy into motivation to keep preparing.

So, let's get started; it's time to get to work!

*fig. 2: Visual Overview of Introduction and Structure

Firefighter Rule Book: Winning Answers Framework Overview

TopScore Top5
This five-part system is designed to allow candidates to construct dynamic and winning answers to the Real Questions portion of interview. The Job Interview Rule Book thoroughly explains The TopScore Top5 and its components:
1) Full Answer to Question
2) Personal History
3) Personal Story
4) Department Knowledge
5) Keywords

Marketing Priorities
Marketing Priorities are your personal highlights that communicate your positive attributes, skill, and potential to the organization.
1) Life highlights that ensure uniquely personalized answers.
2) Communicates personal traits and skills not immediately evident on résumé.
3) Blended with TopScore Top5 for dynamic answers.

Core Values
Core Values are your fundamental beliefs and guiding principles that dictate your behavior and actions.
1) Knowing, defining, and communicating your Core Values ensures thorough and principle-based answers.
2) Core Values are blended with Marketing Priorities using the TopScore Top5 system. resulting in a fluid, rich answer.

The Rules
The Rules govern all parts of the Interview Process—the application process, actual interview, and the interview follow-up. We reveal over 70 rules—even the unspoken—that are often the difference between securing a position or continuing the job hunt.

Chapter 1
Getting Started

In this chapter you'll learn:

    A. The Application Process
    B. Written Tests
    C. Physical Aptitude Tests

Rules: This chapter includes two Rules to help you successfully apply topics A-C listed above.

A: The Application Process

Before we discuss the interview, let's take a few minutes to describe the process that comes before landing the oral interview.

Securing a position with a Fire Department is a competitive, challenging process, so be prepared to step outside what is considered "normal" for landing a nine-to-five job. If you are a competitive person, embrace the process. If you are not, you'll have to motivate yourself to become so.

Rule: Research the department.

Rule: Talk to the newest members to see what the department is looking for.

Your first step to getting hired with a Fire Department is identifying which departments are hiring. There are subscription-based websites that will post hiring notices for the areas you are interested in. The number of candidates hired and the frequency of hiring differ from department to department. Most of the larger departments will establish an eligibility list for their fire academies and draw from them as the need arises. Other departments may hire individually; however, these departments might require a current firefighter and/or Emergency Medical Technician certification.

The standard process for applying to be a new recruit normally begins with submitting an interest card or registering, which then proceeds to a written test. Following the written test, a number of candidates will be eliminated while the remaining members proceed to either a physical aptitude test or an oral interview.

Interest cards and important hiring information can be accessed on the department website. Ensure that you are aware of any extra requirements needed to apply.

Once you overcome these hurdles, the candidates either go to a chief's interview or are rank-ordered according to their scores for hiring on an as-needed basis. This rank order is usually held for a certain predetermined amount of time, and when this time has expired, the list is scrubbed and the whole process begins again. Some Fire Departments have their own training academies, while others utilize outsourced academies that may be required to apply for an entry position. Check with your desired department to confirm the prerequisites required for the job as well as the hiring process in general.

B: Written Test

The written test separates the wheat from the chaff. Contact the HR department and ask if they have published the test format and/or which company is providing the test you will be taking. Then, find a book or website to prepare for the specific test.

A local department brought in over 600 applicants for 10 jobs. The hiring prior to that one brought in thousands. The reduced number of applicants during the second hiring resulted from a newly implemented requirement to be EMT certified. Yes, it is that competitive, so study up!

C: Physical Aptitude Test

The Physical Aptitude Test is just what the name implies: physical, in which you will be required to conduct numerous physical maneuvers in a certain amount of time. The most common Physical Aptitude Test is the CPAT test. However, some departments opt to use a department developed agility test instead. Most end up being similar to the CPAT while some instead use Functional Movement Screenings in combination with another physical test such as a mile-and-a-half run in 11 minutes, 30 seconds.

Whatever test your specific department chooses, you will need to be in your top physical shape, so start preparing now. This is most likely a pass/fail event. Failing by even a second could cost you the job. Once again, check with the local HR Department to discover what is entailed in their physical assessment.

Chapter 1 Review
Putting it into Play

Consider the following to review Chapter 1.

1) Which departments are hiring? How many candidates are they hiring? How frequently do they hire? Do they hire from a fire academy or individually? What are the individual department requirements and certifications?
2) Review the department's website. Note the important hiring dates. Do they require an interest card or some other form of registration? Complete the initial application steps.
3) Research your targeted department's written test. Contact the HR Department, ask if they have published the test format and/or which company is providing the test you will be taking; then, find a book or website to prepare for the specific test.
4) Research your department's Physical Aptitude Test. Contact the HR Department or interview a current Fire Department member for specifics regarding the Physical Aptitude Tests. Start a workout routine now.

Chapter 2
Oral Interview Preparation

In this chapter you'll learn:

- A. Overview
- B. Interview Preparation
- C. Learn the Job Description
- D. Your First Impression
- E. Your Second Impression
- F. Dress for Success
- G. Question Types
  - Real Questions
  - What If/Hypothetical Questions

Rules: This chapter includes five Rules to help you successfully apply topics A-G listed above.

A: Interview Overview

If you have made it to an oral interview, you have distinguished yourself above many other candidates, but do not make the mistake of becoming complacent. Your true grit will be exposed now, and it remains fiercely competitive. Look for any and all opportunities to improve yourself. It could be a fraction of a percent separating you from attaining your dream or looking for the next test.

One of the greatest attributes of being a firefighter is the ability to show up at the scene of a fire and immediately go right to work. The homeowner completely trusts you to handle the situation. There is no interview process and definitely no need to sell yourself.

However, prior to achieving this status, landing the job will require you to perfect the art of selling yourself. No one is going to shout out your accomplishments from the top of a mountain about what a phenomenal asset you will be for the department. It's up to you!

The most successful salespeople are individuals who wholeheartedly believe in the product they are selling. This means you need to believe, to your core, that you are the best investment for the department for which you are testing. Who better to present an overwhelming positive view of your abilities and capabilities to the interview board? When you effectively sell yourself to the board, it will leave no doubt in their minds that you will be a tremendous asset, not only now, but 20 years into your career.

Yes, this is uncomfortable for most individuals. You must overcome these nagging doubts and prepare yourself to impart a convincing and outstanding presentation to the oral panel. It takes lots of work, but it's worth it!

The interview board will ask a wide range of questions with a specific objective. They want to get to know you to the best of their ability, and identify whether you will fit the department. The interview board is looking for more than just whether you're a person who is easy to get along with; they want to know if they can depend on you and whether they can trust you with their lives. You need to know and understand you are interviewing to be part of a family—their family. Always speak from your heart, stay positive, and focus on your successes in life.

Firefighters must be able to respond quickly and coordinate their activities as part of a highly effective team. They must have excellent communication skills and exercise compassion, dignity, and respect, whether on the scene of an emergency, out with the public, or back at the station.

Moving forward, we'll dig deeper into exactly how to identify and sell your top traits.

B: Interview Preparation

Start by clearly identifying your goal. Write it down and post it where you will see it every day. Reading your goal and visualizing your success will help keep you motivated. You can't afford to be average. When people call on the Fire Department, they don't want someone average showing up at their door. Firefighters need to prepare for anything at any time. **The public expects you to have the tools to answer their calls. Your interview panel shares the same mindset.**

They expect you to meet the objectives set forth in the questions they ask.

Interview preparation consists of five parts:

1. Education: First, you need to understand the interview process, what the interview board is looking for and how to approach the interview. You'll cover that by reading the rest of the book.
2. Research: Next, you'll need to do research about the department and city.
3. Groundwork: Throughout the book, you'll be given tasks to help you recall your Personal Story and skills, which you will include in your interview.
4. Organization: Once you've done your research and brain dump, you'll organize your answers following the TopScore system.
5. Practice: Finally, you'll practice. The general rule is treat preparation like a part-time job. Most successful candidates spend upwards of 50 hours preparing for their interview.

As you move forward, keep this in mind: You are more marketable than you give yourself credit for. Often, we do not give ourselves the respect and acknowledgment we deserve. In many cases, we are our own worst enemy. In practice or during an interview, do not downplay your experience, accomplishments, or accreditations. If you have very little work history and life experience, dig through your past for any relevant experience. The fact you delivered pizza for a summer can highlight that you are familiar with the city's address breaks, not to mention knowing how navigate the streets.

Rule: The candidates most prepared for their interview perform the best.

C: Learn the Job Description

An important part of interview preparation is a thorough knowledge of the department's job description. It is not only necessary to know the position you are testing for, but also critical to let the board know you clearly understand the expectations set before you. Do not allow television shows or movies to be your impression of what a professional firefighter is. The majority of firefighter job descriptions are going to be similar no matter where you apply but look for subtle differences in the description and plan to bring them up in a positive way during your interview.

The following is an example from a small section of the Mesa Fire Department's job description. This was taken from the City of Mesa's (AZ) website in October 2013. Most departments' job descriptions will look something like this:

> Entry Level Mesa Firefighter Job Description
>
> Overview: Firefighters must be able to respond quickly and coordinate their activities as an effective team. This work requires attention to detail as well as skill in communication with compassion, dignity, and respect.
>
> Classification Responsibilities: Firefighters perform public safety work involving the protection of life and property by fighting fires, responding to emergency incidents, using Emergency Medical Services (EMS) skills, and engaging in fire code enforcement, public education, and station and equipment maintenance activities. This class is responsible for performing related duties as required.
>
> Distinguishing Features: Upon successful completion of the Mesa Firefighter - Recruit Academy and completion of the criteria for promotion, Firefighter - Recruits are criteria-based promoted to the Firefighter classification. Firefighters are required to work 24-hour shifts and 56-hour work weeks, and may be assigned to work a day assignment (40-hour work week) while assisting on special projects. Work is at the fire station and scenes of fires.
>
> QUALIFICATIONS
>
> Minimum Qualification(s) Required. Must meet the qualifications and special requirements for Firefighter Recruit. Must successfully complete the Mesa Firefighter-Recruit Training Academy and criteria for promotion to Firefighter. Possession of current State of Arizona Emergency Medical Technician (EMT) certification.
>
> Preferred/Desirable Qualification(s). Coursework toward an Associate's Degree in Fire Science or Fire Science Technology from a regionally accredited college or university is preferred. Bilingual in Spanish is desirable.

ESSENTIAL FUNCTIONS

Communication: Communicates with the general public and other City employees in performing community service and public education activities, conducting business inspections, presenting public safety training classes, participating in school programs, answering questions, delivering emergency care, and ensuring patient needs. Produces written documents to document technical and legal matters.

Manual/Physical: Responds to emergency incidents, fights fires, and utilizes either basic life support (BLS) or advanced life support (ALS) and/or paramedic skills. Uses firefighting equipment, including fire hoses or apparatus at emergency incidents. Assists in advancing hose lines and making hydrant connections. Operates the following: hydraulic or pneumatic rescue equipment to rescue trapped or endangered persons and to force entry into locked vehicles or structures; fire apparatus during fire suppression activities. Uses axes, pry tools, and pike poles to enter vehicles or structures. Uses common hand tools to overhaul a fire scene and perform routine fire apparatus maintenance duties. Performs searches and rescues inside burning buildings.

Moves heavy objects (up to 185 pounds or more) including 5-inch fire hoses, EMS equipment, salvage equipment, smoke ejectors, trauma boxes and body boards for short distances (150 feet or less) with the assistance of an aid, in performing firefighting and related duties.

The duties listed above are intended only as general illustrations of the various types of work that may be performed. Specific statements of duties not included do not exclude them from the position if the work is similar, related, or a logical assignment to the position. Job descriptions are subject to change by the City as the needs of the City and requirements of the job change.

As you can see, there are numerous details to the entry-level firefighter position. The more details in the job description, the more opportunities you have to highlight your similar qualifications and abilities.

This particular job description emphasizes the arduous physical tasks and heavy lifting a firefighter is required to perform. It would be beneficial to bring up your involvement in physical fitness activities and how you have been dedicated to a fit lifestyle. The document also states the candidate will be performing public training, speaking at public safety classes, and speaking to groups at fire-related school programs. This would be an instance when you want to highlight that you have performed in public speaking and that you have volunteered with children. If you have any experience with speaking Spanish, you would want to communicate this in your interview, as well.

D: Your First Impression

Rule: Make a good first impression.

Rule: Bring enough résumés for everyone on the board to have copies, plus a couple extra.

The oral board's first impression of you occurs well before you ever walk into the interview room. You are probably saying, "What?" but it is true. Your application and résumé will provide the first impression, and (not to sound cliché) no one gets a second chance to make a first impression. Your application and résumé should highlight your skills and abilities in a manner that causes the oral board to form a positive view of you well before they ever meet you.

Applications are primarily completed online but may or may not reach the oral panel. It is still important for them to be filled out properly so have your application proofread before submitting it.

A résumé, on the other hand, is reviewed by the oral panel and can either help or hurt you prior to your interview. The résumé needs to be professional, one page, and should highlight your greatest assets. A cover letter will not be needed. While these are the general rules, check the specific job announcement for special instructions.

There are multiple résumé templates online that are professional, easy to use, and best of all: free! Try searching the Google Docs Template Gallery, and you will find multiple templates available; select one that best represents you. When your résumé is done, try taping it up on the wall, and then take a few steps back to where you can no longer read the words. Look at the spacing and aesthetics. Ask yourself the following:

1. Is my résumé balanced?
2. Are my headings and font/style selections consistent?
3. Are my margins even?
4. Does this document represent me from an aesthetic viewpoint?

Once you are satisfied with the appearance of the résumé, make sure that you scrutinize it for typos, grammar, and spelling errors. When you think it is polished, it is a good idea to wait one day, and then look at it with fresh eyes.

Purchase quality résumé paper in a neutral shade, and print enough copies for all involved in the interview. Imagine you are on the panel and you have seen 300 résumés, all on the same white, boring paper. Then you get a professional résumé on quality paper. Is it going to stand out? Is it going to show effort and look better than any other résumé?

Whenever possible, submit your résumé before your interview. But, always bring additional copies.

E: Second Impression

(Your first visible impression)

Rule: Make a good impression.

Your second impression begins the moment you walk through the door for the interview. In order to prepare adequately, you must visualize and practice this essential moment. You need to enter the room with enthusiasm and confidence, look the panelists in the eyes, smile, and give firm handshakes. A proper entry and introduction will get everything moving in the right direction. Do your best to remember their names and ranks. This will also help ensure that your follow-up thank you cards will reach the correct people. We'll talk more about that later.

Wait for a member of the oral board to invite you to take a seat. If the chair is 20 feet away from the table, ask to move it closer while being careful not to invade the board members' personal space. Once seated, be aware that your body position and posture continue to display confidence and respect. Simple body language, such as placing your elbows on the table or slouching, will send the wrong message. Studies show the spoken word accounts for approximately 8-35 percent of the message we are trying to convey (depending on the study referenced). This means that the remaining 65-92 percent is communicated non-verbally. Wow!

Amy Cuddy, a Social Psychologist and Associate Professor of Business Administration at Harvard Business School and keynote speaker on body language, gave a talk at the June 2012 TED Talk Convention, where she addresses how body language affects the way people are viewed by others and how to change others' perception of you. At the time of this book's publication, the video had over 40 million views. Find it on YouTube and watch it now, and then again before your interview. Process the information and visualize entering the room for the oral interview; practice that moment multiple times before the actual interview.

F: Dress for Success

Rule: Dress like a professional.

It is simple: This is a job for professionals by professionals, so dress appropriately. Wear conservative business attire such as a dark-colored suit with a white or gray shirt. A tie is a necessity for men. Women should wear knee-length skirts (or longer) or business slacks with matching blouses. Neither gender should wear excessive jewelry. Avoid bright colors and distracting shirt or tie patterns. Remember, dress the part of a professional.

G: Question Types

There will be two types of questions during your interview: Real Questions and What If Questions.

- Real Questions deal with specific events and accomplishments you have accumulated throughout your life. To answer these types of questions, you'll use the TopScore Top5 with your Marketing Priorities and Core Values interwoven within your answer. These are all covered in the following chapters.
- Example Real Questions: Why do you want to be a firefighter? Tell me about a time you had a conflict at work and how you handled it.
- What If Questions deal with hypothetical situations. The oral board wants to judge your reaction and subsequent action to what are most likely uncomfortable situations. What If Questions include Situational, Leading, and Interpersonal questions. The interview board will ask a wide range of questions with a specific objective designed to get to know you to the best of their ability and to identify whether you will fit their department.

- Example What If Questions: An officer asks you to go into a building that you know will put you and your team in danger. What to you do?

Chapter 2 Review
Putting it Into Play

Consider the following to review the content presented in Chapter 2

1) Clearly identify your goal, write it down, and post it where you will see it every day. Create a smaller Goal Card, and keep it with you to help keep you motivated and focused throughout the day.
2) Start a list of your personal attributes you believe you can sell. Ask those closest to you for attributes that you may have overlooked. Think of Personal Stories that will help you sell those attributes to an interview board. Practice selling yourself to people who know you; ask for help in remaining authentic.
3) Locate and print the job description of your targeted department. Analyze the job description for the small details and attributes they are looking for. List those on paper and try to match tangible evidence of those qualities and details from your personal life and experience.
4) Watch Amy Cuddy's TED Talk: "Your Language May Shape Who You Are." Take notes and practice her positive body language. Visualize and practice entering a room with an interview board. Ask people you know to help you role play this scenario. Ask for their feedback and observations regarding your presence and body language.
5) Select an interview outfit and hang it where you can see it every day. This will also help keep you focused and motivated.

Chapter 3
TopScore Top5 System

In this chapter you'll learn:

A. TopScore Top5 Overview
B. TopScore Top5 Components:
   1. Answer the Question
   2. Personal History (PH)
   3. Personal Story (PS)
   4. Department Knowledge (DK)
   5. Keywords (KW)

Rules: This chapter includes seven Rules to help you successfully apply topics A-B listed above.

A: TopScore Top5 Overview

Rule: Utilize the TopScore Top5 to answer ALL Real Questions.

The TopScore Top5 provides the foundation to answer the Real Questions portion of the interview. Remember from Chapter One, Real Questions ask about you, your history, and look for examples to back up your character claims and skills.

When answering a Real Question, keep in mind you must not simply answer the question. Everyone answers the question. To get the job you must be different than everyone else and provide an answer to help the department know more about you and show what you know about the department. Think of it this way; like in school, doing what is required earns you a C. Going above and beyond earns you an A. To get a job with a Fire Department, you must earn the A and do all of the extra credit.

In order to give an excellent answer, you must first get into the head of the interview board and understand why they ask the questions they do. During this section of the interview, the board intentionally chooses questions to engage you and to judge your eagerness, ability, and suitability for the job.

The important items you add to support your answers are what will get you hired.

By adding the following five parts to every answer, you will cut out 90 percent of your competition and provide the interview board with the information they need to confidently offer you the job.

Every answer should include:

1. Answer to the Question
2. Personal History
3. Personal Story
4. Department Knowledge
5. Keywords

During an average interview, you will have between four and eight Real Questions to answer in about 30 minutes. This time will allow you to elaborate on your answers and allow the board to get to know you. The people who simply provide a basic answer to the question will be finished with their interview in five minutes.

For example, if there are eight questions, and you reply with five pieces of your Personal History in every answer, the board will know 40 more things about you! This will make their decision to hire you a lot easier. Thirty minutes is not a lot of time to get to know somebody who you are going to spend the next 25 years with. Think of the things you would want to know if you were getting married (spending the next 25-plus years with someone) and you had 3,000 applicants, each having 30 minutes to answer your questions. You would pick the ones that gave you the most information about themselves (Personal History), spoke your language (Keywords), who were able to tell you stories you will not forget (Personal Story), and who included why they would be a perfect fit based on their expert knowledge of you (Department Knowledge). Provide the oral board with the information they need to choose you as the best candidate.

The TopScore Top5 provides structure to your response and will prevent you from rambling. When you have hit all five parts of your answer, you are done! The hardest part is learning how to segue from one part of your answer to the other to make it sound natural and fluid. The TopScore Top5 does not necessarily need to be addressed in any particular order, but each of these aspects must be addressed to receive a top score for your answer.

For example: If you face a simple question, such as "What is your favorite color?"

If you simply answer "blue," you will not get hired.

You need to give the board enough information to understand why you chose blue.

Instead, answer:

> Blue has been my favorite color as long as I can remember. My first **(PH)** hockey jersey was a blue Hartford Whalers jersey. Playing with the Whalers was how I learned the value of the **(KW)** teamwork and **(KW)** camaraderie associated with being part of a winning team. My friends and I were not the best players in the league, but we played as a team. We worked together toward the same goal, and we managed to win the **(PH)** championship in 2008. **(PS)** I can still remember the great feeling of skating around and passing the trophy from teammate to teammate, plus the fun we had at the celebration afterward. I have played team sports my entire life. I grew up playing **(PH)** soccer and then transitioned to **(PH)** football and eventually **(PH)** ice hockey.
>
> I know the Fire Department is one big team and gains from the **(KW)** strength of all involved. Working as a team can be **(KW)** safer, faster, and more enjoyable than working alone. I know from my ride-alongs that your Fire Department has many teams like the **(DK)** four-person engine and **(DK)** six-person truck companies. You also have **(DK)** Dive, **(DK)** Tech, **(DK)** Hazmat, and **(DK)** Aircraft Rescue Firefighting teams. I would be honored to be part of this **(KW)** progressive department, and I look forward to joining one of your specialty teams in the future.

Despite the simplicity of the question about your favorite color, good use of the TopScore Top5 will tell the oral board exactly what they need to know about you. The sample answer above told the board a host of information. The board now knows that you play hockey, you work well in a team environment, you enjoy the camaraderie of working together, and that you are able to obtain goals through synergy. The board learned all of this by simply listening to you explain why blue is your favorite color.

Let's look at another common question.

Odds are, you will be asked a question similar to, "Tell us about yourself." This is a Real Question and an icebreaker.

The board wants to know a little about you. Have you traveled the world? Is there something unique about your story? Is there something they need to know that will not be revealed in the general questions?

Make them want to get to know you more and look forward to your answers. Add teasers like, "One year I took a three-year trip to Antarctica, and I hope I can elaborate on that later." Talk about what you take pride in and your life experience.

Start out smiling and speak energetically. Show you are excited to be there and that you are happy and friendly. This sets the tone for your interview. When you start out speaking confidently and comfortably, you will feel better moving forward.

Introduce your number one Marketing Priority here and follow it up with something like, "I look forward to talking more about that experience during this interview." We'll talk more about your Marketing Priorities later in the book.

Other icebreaker questions may include: Why do you want to be a firefighter? What have you done to prepare? Share about who you are. All have the same intended purpose.

B. TopScore Top5 Components

Let's dig into each of the five components. To reiterate, the TopScore Top5 approach applies only to Real Questions and your answer should include:

1. Answer the Question and doing so include the following:
2. Personal History (PH) 3-5 pieces
3. Personal Story (PS) 1 story
4. Department Knowledge (DK) 3-5 pieces
5. Keywords (KW) 3-5 pieces

1) Answer the Question

Rule: Answer the question, the whole question. This might seem obvious, but part of the answer can often be missed. Some questions are multiple-part questions in which interviewees fail to answer all parts of the question.

Restate a multiple-part question back to the board so that you, yourself, hear what you need to cover in your answer. It also provides for good two-way communication. Don't hesitate to ask the board to repeat the question to be sure you didn't miss a part.

For Example:

> Question: Tell the board a time when you faced a challenge in life in which you learned a valuable lesson and how it affected you as a person.
>
> You would repeat: A time I faced a challenge in which I learned a valuable lesson was…. The effect it has on my life was huge. It … and then continue with the TopScore Top5.

2) Personal History

Rule: Get your fishing lines in the water.

This is your history: where you were born, where you grew up, schools you attended, degrees you earned, things about your family, certifications and achievements, your hobbies, sports, trades, and job history.

Think of each piece of Personal History as tags and titles you have accomplished throughout your life: student, son/daughter, waiter, soccer player, volunteer, etc. The more fishing lines you put in the water, the better your chances of hooking something. In an interview, you know you've "hooked something" when you get an oral board member to relate with you. This is the first step in building any relationship. If you talk about things the board can relate to, they will naturally form a bond and view you as a likely candidate to hire. Don't get discouraged when they don't give any indications of connecting with you; it's all part of the test.

For example:

> Growing up as the son of a firefighter, I was always interested in listening to what my father would tell me when he came home from his shift at the firehouse. The stories that had me most interested were stories of how he was able to help someone during their time of need. My young mind often viewed my father in the light of a superhero. These were my first memorable exposures to the job of a firefighter; little did I know that my father's stories planted the seeds for the career path that I would choose to pursue.

Salesmanship requires you to show your enthusiasm, passion, positive attitude, and compassion. Stay away from negativity or showing political or religious opinions or prejudices. Good salesmanship builds and cultivates relationships. When this happens, connecting those Personal History fishing lines to the members on the board becomes natural, and you are guaranteed to have a more favorable score. Remember, the more lines in the water, the better your chances of catching something.

Let's look at a real-life example of relating to the oral board:

A friend and I went to an interview at a local Fire Department. We had both just graduated—Jeff as second and me as first in our college fire academy. Going into this interview, I thought I had it in the bag and just knew I was going to score higher than Jeff. While talking after the interview, I expressed how well I felt I had done. Jeff said his interview was a bit different. The interview was going as expected, and then he mentioned he had a 1965 Mustang that he just finished restoring. As chance would have it, one of the captains across the table had the exact same Mustang. They spent the rest of the interview talking about their cars, where to get parts for their cars and trading technical tips. Guess who got the job? Jeff!

Simply stated, if the oral board can relate to you, it is much easier for them to picture you as the ideal firefighter they desire to have as part of their team. It is easier to work with people who share common interests with you.

You never know what the board will relate with so get those fishing lines in the water!

GROUNDWORK: Write down your top 30 or more things you want the board to know about you. This is your Personal History (PH).

1.	16.
2.	17.
3.	18.
4.	19.
5.	20.
6.	21.
7.	22.
8.	23.
9.	24.
10.	25.
11.	26.
12.	27.
13	28.
14.	29.
15.	30.

3) Personal Story

Rule: Tell stories they will remember.

Think of your Personal History as the words and your Personal Story as the action.

You need to stand out to the oral board, a solid Personal Story makes that happen. You convince the board of your skills, not when you claim them, but when you demonstrate them. Actions speak louder than words. Your stories work to make you more memorable AND serve as evidence to your claims; both are things you'll need to get the job offer.

The Personal Story you choose to tell should support your Personal History. For instance, if you talk about being a good leader, you should have a good Personal Story to back it up. It will usually start with something like, "One time I..." or "I remember when I..." This is where you will employ your Marketing Strategies interlaced with Core Values. We will cover these later in the book; they will help you narrow down your valuable stories.

Keep in mind, your story should provide enough information to engage the interview board but not have so much detail that you bore them. Include only the details that support your main point and leave out anything else.

4) Department Knowledge

Rule: Look on the internet for useful information about the department. Do ride-alongs to find crucial details not available on the web.

Of course, you want to be a firefighter, but why do you want to be a firefighter with this particular department? Department knowledge displays your interest in the department you are interviewing for—their department! Firefighters who work, live, breathe, sweat, and bleed together have a tremendous amount of pride and appreciation for what their department accomplishes on a daily basis.

Showing ample Department Knowledge accomplishes two things. First, it demonstrates interest in and commitment to your future department. It proves that you've embraced the challenge and you take your future job seriously; it shows sincerity and a commitment to be a part of the department's team. Second, it will help to ensure that you've selected the department best suited for you. Talk about the department's strategic plan and include the department's mission statement in your answers.

> For example: "I believe in Backdraft Fire Department's mission statement, which states, "...". Therefore, I would "...".

A way to learn the specifics about a department is to schedule a ride-along. A ride-along provides an opportunity to learn about the department at a deeper level than you can from the Internet. Schedule them. You'll learn more rules about the ride-along later in the book.

It is also important to have a good understanding of general fire history. You need to become a student of all aspects of the profession. Learn who started the fire service and why. What is the Maltese Cross and how did it become the badge of the fire service? Why are fire trucks painted red? How and where did fire poles come about? Learn the facts and figures about the Fire Department to which you are applying, as well as the fire service in general, and you will give yourself one more edge over the competition.

Finally, do research about the city the department serves. How many citizens does it serve? Who is the Mayor?

During your online research, start with the following questions:

- Who is the department Chief, and what is their history in the department?
- What is the population of the area the department serves?
- How many square miles does it serve?
- How many stations?
- How many engine companies?
- How many truck companies?

GROUNDWORK: Write down 20 significant facts regarding your Fire Department.

1.
2.
3.
4.
5.
6.
7.
8.
9.
10.
11.
12.
13.
14.
15.
16
17.
18.
19.
20.

5) Keywords

Rule: Use Keywords, especially words popular with the department.

Keywords are terms a Fire Department holds in high esteem. When you use Keywords, you start speaking the board's language. Every time you use a Keyword, the interviewers' brains reengage. Often, they consider them so important they will make note of each time you use one.

You will find these Keywords in the department's mission statement, strategic plan, job description, and/or recruitment guidelines. Look for words like: teamwork, family, leadership, dedication, pride, service, etc. Use these important Keywords to summarize your experience and accomplishments. Keywords provide an opportunity to tell the board more about you. Each Keyword must have substance behind it.

Below you'll find a few examples of Keywords. Do your research and find more, especially those specifically meaningful to your department. These definitions are blended from Merriam-Webster's, Wikipedia, and Dictionary.com as well as TopScore preference when applied within the scope of the fire service.

Pride - a high or inordinate opinion of one's own dignity, importance, merit, or superiority, whether as cherished in the mind or as displayed in bearing, conduct, etc.

Respect - Esteem for or a sense of the worth or excellence of a person; a personal quality or ability or something considered as a manifestation of a personal quality or ability.

Integrity - Consistency of actions, values, methods, measures, and principles. Depth and breadth of a value system may also be significant factors due to their congruence with a wider range of observations. People have integrity to the extent that they behave according to the values, beliefs, and principles they claim to hold. One's value system may evolve over time while retaining integrity if inconsistencies are accounted for and resolved. Hypocrisy results when one part of a value system is demonstrably at odds with another, and the person or group of people holding those values fails to account for the discrepancy. Hypocrisy is the opposite of integrity.

Dedication - A feeling of very strong support for or loyalty to someone or something.

Excellence - The state or quality of excelling, particularly in the field of business and organizations. Excellence is considered an important value and a goal to be pursued.

Leadership - The position or function of a leader, a person who guides or directs a group.

Accountability - In leadership roles, accountability is the acknowledgment and assumption of responsibility for actions, products, decisions, and policies including the administration, governance, and implementation within the scope of the role or employment position. This encompasses the obligation to report, explain, and be answerable for resulting consequences.

Responsibility - The state or fact of being responsible, answerable or accountable for something within one's power, control or management.

Chain of Command - A series of administrative or military ranks, positions, etc., in which each has direct authority over the one immediately below.

Camaraderie - A spirit of familiarity and trust existing between friends.

Tolerance - A fair, objective, and permissive attitude toward those whose opinions, practices, race, religion, nationality, etc., differ from one's own. Freedom from bigotry.

Loyalty - Faithful to one's oath, commitments, or obligations.

Fair - Free from bias, dishonesty, or injustice.

Flexibility - A personality trait; the extent to which a person can cope with changes in circumstances and think about problems and tasks in novel, creative ways. This trait is used when stressors or unexpected events occur, requiring a person to change his or her stance, outlook, or commitment.

Reliability - Consistently good in quality or performance; able to be trusted.

Honesty- Being able to be trusted for one's word.

Motivation - Interest in or enthusiasm for doing something.

Positive Attitude - Displaying a positive state of mind or feeling.

Professionalism - The level of excellence or competence expected from a professional.

Team Oriented - Team oriented means you don't think of just yourself. You include others in your decisions. Everyone has a contributing factor in the operations and decisions.

Trust - Firm reliance on the integrity, ability, or character of another person.

Selfless Service - Putting the needs of others before one's own.

Compassion - Deep awareness of the suffering of another coupled with the wish to relieve it.

Attitude - The manner in which someone carries oneself.

Respect - Showing admiration for someone based on his or her abilities, qualities or achievements.

Responsibility/Accountability - A form of trustworthiness; the trait of being answerable to someone for something or being responsible for one's conduct.

Excellence - A state of possessing good qualities to an eminent degree; exalted merit; superiority in virtue.

Empowerment - Knowledge of and faith in one's own ability.

Humility - Freedom from arrogance.

Success - The achievement of something desired, planned, or attempted.

Exceed: To be better than. Go beyond what is expected.

Mentor - An influential counselor, coach, or leader

Comply - To act accordingly; follow directions or a direct order

Generate - To cause to come about

Excel - Being exceptionally good and proficient in a subject or talent

Summary

The length of your answer can very, as long as you provide an adequate amount of information for the board to get to know you. Strong answers tend to be between four and seven minutes long.

Don't be discouraged; the first few times you try this you may sound robotic. It takes practice to make your answers sound natural and fluid. In the next chapter, we'll put this all into play and walk through several examples.

Chapter 3 Review
Putting it into Play

Consider the following to review the content presented in Chapter 3.

Return to Chapter 3 and complete all the provided lists. Keep these for the next practice section, which will ask you to complete full TopScore Top5 answers to Real Questions.

1. Write down 20 significant facts regarding your Fire Department.
2. Write down your top 30 or more things you want the board to know about you, your Personal History.

Chapter 4
Real Questions
and Example Answers

In this chapter you'll review three Real Questions and answers:

A. What impact does stress and pressure have on a person's decision-making skills?
B. What is the most important trait a firefighter must have and why?
C. Explain to the board what you consider a personal weakness.

Overview:

Real Questions will probably be asked first in your interview. Below are examples of Real Questions and possible answers. We've identified the parts of the TopScore Top5 in the first answer so you can see how it all comes together. In the next one, you'll get an opportunity to identify the parts. This isn't a time filler exercise. It's designed to help you commit all five parts to memory so your brain naturally fills in the gaps when you build your own answers.

A: Real Question Example 1

What impact does stress and pressure have on a person's decision-making skills?

TopScore Answer:

Stress and pressure will stimulate a person in one of two ways: negatively or positively. Negative stimulation will result in a poor decision or can lead to quick decisions, resulting in both mistakes or compromising **(KW)** safety.

My senior year of high school, I took an early EMT course **(PH)**. It was a highly coveted class because the top scoring students would have the opportunity to compete for a very rare high school internship during our second semester. After a lot of dedication

(KW), I was selected to compete for the internship. Unfortunately, I froze under the pressure. It was a simple skill I had passed hundreds of times that semester. I practiced the skill over and over, but the one thing I didn't account for was stress. Although I didn't get *that* internship, I did learn a valuable lesson: My skills are useless unless I can deploy them under stress. It became my goal to improve my reaction to stress.

After landing a different internship **(PH)** with a local transport company, I started talking to experienced first responders. There, I saw how a positive reaction to stress could make people more efficient. When people are trained to operate during times of high stress and are equipped with the proper tools for the job, their **(KW)** situational awareness is high. **(DK)** Here at Backdraft Fire Department, the training department is recognized as one of the best in the state. **(DK)** Backdraft Fire Department recognizes and makes training a high priority within the department. More importantly, you train members to learn how to deal with and work in stressful situations.

(PS) Last summer, while dining at a local restaurant, a gentleman who was sitting a few tables away from me suffered a major heart attack. A person nearby witnessed the event and rushed over to the unconscious man and started a quick assessment. He then told a customer to call 9-1-1. Little did I know, the **(PH)** CPR training I completed five years earlier during my senior year of high school was about to be put to the test. I sprang from my chair without hesitation and assisted the bystander with moving the patient to the floor. The bystander asked me if I knew CPR and I responded, "Yes, I do." He told me to perform chest compressions. I kneeled beside the patient and without even thinking, I located the notch where the lower part of the rib meets the center of the chest and began counting as I compressed the patient's chest. I continued compressions for five minutes until the Fire Department arrived on scene. Obviously, this went from a calm night having dinner to a very significant and stressful event. That evening I learned a lot about how I would respond in a stressful situation. I had previous **(KW)** training, albeit five years prior, and despite the passage of time, I had perfect memory recall and was able to stay focused and calm while performing CPR.

I don't believe a person's response to stress is purely biological. I'm confident that through training, exposure, and diligence anyone can positively react in stressful situations. This is the number one reason I take training seriously. As I once heard, "You're only as good as your best day of training."

Let's examine the response above to see what aspects of the TopScore Top5 were addressed:

1. Answer the Question: The question was answered, and a positive spin was put on it.
2. Personal History: Taking an EMT class in high school, landing an internship after not giving up, CPR certified.
3. Personal Story: Performing CPR while out at dinner.
4. Keywords: Situational awareness, safety, training, dedication.
5. Department Knowledge: Talking about the training department being recognized as one of the best in the state demonstrates you have studied this specific department.

B: Real Question Example 2

What is the most important trait a firefighter must have and why?

This is an example of a two-part question and requires two complete answers, as well as each of the additional TopScore parts. Try to identify each part of the TopScore Top5.

Top Score Answer:

I believe the most important trait a firefighter must have is ( ) integrity. It is the foundation of every trait a firefighter must exhibit. It is the trait or value, which defines our character. A person with ( ) integrity, is committed to being ( ) honest, ( ) dependable, ( ) respectful and ( ) dedicated. ( ) All vital traits to maintaining an effective Fire Department.

During several ride-alongs with Backdraft Fire Department, I saw how Backdraft Firefighters ( ) exemplify this trait. It was impossible not to notice their personal dedication ( ) and their dedication to their crew, their community and their department. I have seen and respect the ( ) integrity and work ethic of the firefighters and the attitude of the department.

During my ride-alongs, I was excited to learn how ( ) progressive this department is. I learned about things your department has to offer such as ( ) Dive, ( ) Hazmat, ( ) Rope, ( ) and Aircraft Rescue teams, as well as a ( ) paramedic program with half of your ( ) 25 stations being advanced life support engines. I believe the only way for a department to advance to this level is by compiling a team defined by integrity ( ).

Integrity is most important because firefighters are entrusted with people's most prized possessions every day. Whether those possessions are the lives of their family members and pets, or home and personal belongings, firefighters must be ( ) trustworthy so that the community can depend on us. We do not have the option of betraying someone's trust. We are firefighters at all times, whether we are on or off duty.

I am ( ) 29 years old with a ( ) wife and ( ) two young kids. I grew up playing team sports like ( ) football and ( ) hockey. I am now in the ( ) construction and remodeling business and often find myself with keys and codes to people's homes. I do not take this responsibility lightly. ( ) The success of my business rides not only on customer satisfaction once the project is complete but also on how I treated them and their home. ( ) A customer may be happy with the outcome of the project, but if they do not trust me or like me as a person, they will never refer me to a friend. My business depends on those referrals. I can tell you this: There is nothing in anyone's home that is worth the price of my integrity. More than anything, stealing and dishonesty are not in my genetic make-up.

( ) Just the other day, I was at one of the local box stores returning a few small items that I did not use on my last remodel. When I handed the cashier the items to scan and return, she told me that they were not on my receipt. I then handed her the debit card I used to purchase the items, and again, she said the items were not purchased on that card. Without proof, the cashier could not give me cash but would have to give me in-store credit instead. She began to set up a gift card for the balance and then it dawned on me: I had the correct receipt and the correct card. I double checked the receipt and realized that I was never charged. I had purchased several items at the same time, and somehow, four items were never scanned. I explained that I had purchased four identical items and had used two, but wanted to return the other two. She asked me what I wanted to do. I told her that I not only needed to decline the gift card, but I also needed to be charged for the two items I used but did not pay for.

I live the ( ) value of ( ) integrity every day of my life, and I understand the importance it plays in life, business and especially the Fire Department. I know I can be counted on to continue the ( ) tradition of ( ) honesty, ( ) integrity and ( ) trustworthiness of this Fire Department.

C. Real Questions Example 3

Explain to the board what you consider as a personal weakness.

Most candidates find this to be one of the most difficult questions to answer. Do not be taken off guard. Be prepared for this question or something similar, such as, "Tell us about a time you failed at work or disobeyed a direct order."

The board isn't surprised you have weaknesses! You're human. What they really want to know is: how do you respond? Do you have grit? Do you take responsibility? Can you overcome? Use your Personal Story to answer those questions. In addition to using the TopScore Top5, remember to keep it positive. As you answer the question about your weakness, address how you are improving.

This time we've removed the TopScore Top5 identification. Make it your goal to include each part naturally. You won't successfully predict your interview questions or memorize your answers. You must be comfortable enough with the system to build your answers on the spot.

TopScore Answer:

> Public speaking is an area I am working to improve. Sitting here in front of you reminds me of a feeling I had before a speech I gave in the fifth grade. I was running for student body vice president, and as I stood in front of my entire grade school ready to give my speech, I completely froze. The kids started to giggle and I stepped away from the podium to gather myself before I tried again. This happened about three times before the principal finally leaned in behind me and whispered, "Why don't you start with your name?" With that suggestion, my speech came back to me. I stepped up to

the microphone and delivered. As it turned out, I won the election. I guess it's mostly about being memorable when you're in elementary school.

Since then, I've gotten a lot more comfortable speaking in front of people, but, in that moment, while I was figuring out public speaking in elementary school, at the back of the auditorium stood both my parents supporting me, just as they had while I practiced the speech over and over. I do not consider my public speaking a strength, but I can assure you it is better than it used to be.

I know Backdraft Fire Department has been teaching Fire Safety since the early 1930s. Teaching 25 first- and second-graders about Stop, Drop, and Roll is something I look forward to. I mentioned that my parents encouraged me back in fifth grade. They continue to do so as they did on the phone this morning prior this interview. Following their example by encouraging others has become second nature for me. Although public speaking is not a strength, I made a commitment to accept the challenge whenever it presents itself. Through practice, I am working to increase my skill and hope to use it to benefit Backdraft Fire.

Chapter 4 Review
Putting it into Play

Consider the following to review the content presented in Chapter 4.

1. Using the following organizer, begin practicing creating TopScore Answers. Start on paper, write out your response, read the response, then move to complete autonomy so your response sounds fluid and natural. Use the sample questions from Part 4 to create your own TopScore Answers.

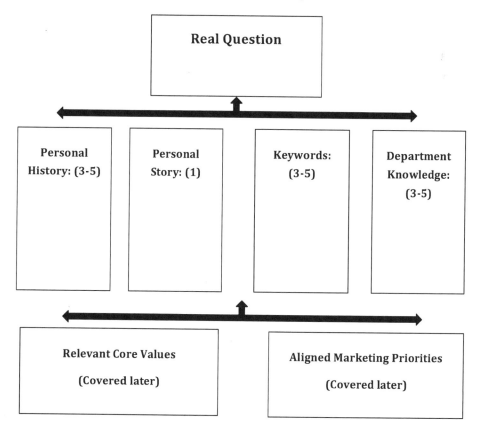

Chapter 5
The "What If" Interview Questions

In this chapter you'll learn:
- A. Overview of What If Questions
- B. Leading Questions
- C. Situational Questions
- D. Interpersonal Questions
- E. Bizarre, Weird, or Just Different Questions

Rules: This chapter includes ten Rules to help you successfully apply topics A-E listed above.

A: The "What If" Questions Overview

In most cases, following the Real Questions, you'll be asked "What If" Questions to gauge how you respond in different situations, how well you interact with others, and your personality. The board will pose a hypothetical situation and then ask a "What If" Question. Something like, "If you saw XYZ happen at the fire station, what would you do?

During "What If" Questions, it is not necessary to use the TopScore Top5 system. There may be appropriate moments to use parts of the TopScore Top5, but it is not necessary to augment your responses with full Personal Stories or Personal Histories.

Rule: Steer the oral board members in the direction you want them to go.

Take the board members or interviewer to the hypothetical world with your answers by engaging with the scenario provided rather than bringing in Personal Stories or Personal History. At times, Keywords and Department Knowledge may be appropriate but don't let your answer get off topic.

It is important not to rush through these questions, even if you have heard the question before and already know exactly what you are going to say. Slow down and act as though you have never heard it before. Rushing through a question might cause you to leave out information that could separate you from the other candidates.

You'll face three types of "What If" Questions that we'll cover individually in each of the following sections.

1. Leading Questions
2. Situational Questions
3. Interpersonal Questions

B: Leading Questions

A Leading Question will attempt to lead you into assuming something negative. Do not take the bait!

Example Leading Question: While on scene of a medical call, you see a fellow firefighter pick up a $20 bill from the kitchen floor. What do you do?

Rule: Don't assume there is a problem. Only assume positive.

By assuming negative, you may be viewed as being untrusting, angry, or not a team player. By assuming positive, you assume that the other firefighters you work with are professional, trustworthy, and acting in the best interest of the Fire Department.

You could start by saying, "Firefighters are known for being honest and trustworthy. I would assume that it just fell out of his pocket."

Rule: Defuse the bomb

Leading Questions are designed to make you assume that something negative is happening, and if you do, you will fail the question. When the board asks you a Leading Question, it's akin to them lighting the fuse to a bomb. If you know how to diffuse it or direct it in a better direction, you will be successful.

Example #1

Leading Question: You see your captain drinking from a flask. What are you going to do?

At this point, the fuse is lit so you must attempt to defuse the bomb.

Response: Yeah, we bought that for him for his birthday. It's our running joke; he keeps water in it.

Now, the bomb is diffused. The board will not let you get away that easy; but they now know you understand the game. The board will then add,

Board Response: You smell alcohol on his breath.

You should continue to assume the positive.

Your Response: This is a job of professionals. If I must trust him with my life, I can trust that he is not drinking on the job. There are other things that could cause his breath to smell of alcohol like cold medicine or mouthwash. I don't think there is a problem.

The board will then give you enough information to show you that something is clearly wrong. In this situation, the person in question is undoubtedly drinking on the job. It is then your responsibility to correct the problem, taking it up the chain of command beginning at the lowest level and continuing until an acceptable outcome is obtained.

Board Response: The Captain is also your father-in-law and is retiring in six months. You know if he is terminated, he will be left with no retirement!

Your follow up on these types of answers must continue to reflect integrity, honor, and devotion to the fire service.

Your Response: I would inform the Captain that it is my obligation to report him to his supervisor since drinking on the job not only poses serious consequences to the firefighter in question, but also to his crew and the citizens we are entrusted to protect. I would also make myself available to provide support and encouragement during this difficult time. It is the very least I could do, family member or not.

By not immediately assuming anything was wrong, you diffused the bomb, which will gain the maximum points available for the question.

Example #2

Leading Question: You see a fellow firefighter taking money out of the cash jar in the soda refrigerator. What do you do?

One approach to take could be that your fellow firefighter probably put a larger bill in the cash jar earlier and was now just making change for it. The interview board might continue the question by adding to the circumstances of the event. Stay positive and only positive until they provide enough information to prove that the firefighter was actually stealing. By staying with positive responses, you can control the direction of your answers. If they provide enough information to prove guilt and illegal actions, you must make sure the issue is addressed and is prosecuted to the fullest extent of the law. You owe it to your department and your profession to do so. Remember, this is a job of professionals by professionals and there is no room for illegal behavior.

Your Response: This is a job of professionals; we need to uphold the public's trust. We are responsible with their lives as well as their property. I should be able to trust my fellow firefighters with my life; surely, I can trust him to get change from a jar on the soda refrigerator.

Notice in the response above that only a positive outcome was assumed. As mentioned earlier, the board might pursue the situation and add to the circumstances of the situation.

Board Response: There has been a lot of money missing.

Your Response: I would make a note of it in my head, but I don't have any proof there is an actual problem. I would trust that the firefighter is doing the right thing until I have concrete proof to the contrary.

You still have the opportunity to assume positive. Because you trust your fellow firefighters, you can trust they will pay it back. At some point in time, the board might state there is actual theft happening at which time you must acknowledge the illegal behavior. You must address the problem and do whatever it takes to rectify the situation using the chain of command that provides the opportunity to deal with any situation at the lowest level possible.

Be prepared to explain how you would address and correct the problem. This piece of the question could be just as important as addressing the leading aspect of the question. When formulating your response, keep in mind the Fire Department is a family and the age-old rule, "treat others as you want to be treated," would apply. You should start by privately and respectfully addressing the issue with the firefighter in question. Wouldn't you expect the same respect from them? Perhaps you'll discover a personal issue provoking this behavior. Regardless of the problem, it's still not acceptable, but it shows compassion and respect and it presents an opportunity for them to rectify the situation before it escalates. This would be an uncomfortable situation, but inform the firefighter in question that he needs to speak with the Captain or Lieutenant (depending on your department), and offer to go with them. If the Captain does not address the situation, take it up the chain to the next highest rank. If the issue is still resolved, keep going up the chain. You know this is not acceptable behavior and it needs to be stopped. Remember, this is more than just a petty theft from a soda jar at the station. Each firefighter is an ambassador of the department and is trusted with the property of taxpayers. Can you imagine the damage to the department's reputation if a firefighter stole from someone they were entrusted to help?

C: Situational Questions

For a Situational Question the board will pose a hypothetical situation with two or more hypothetical outcomes. The board uses Situational Questions to gauge your decision-making ability and confidence. They will try to make you change your mind, but you need to pick a path, justify why you chose it, and stick to it. From the limited information given, either path is correct, but it is important you are able to justify why you picked the path you did. The interview board will make the other path seem very inviting, but do not fall for it! When you are presented with the situation, try to think of another way to accomplish the task; this will have to be a way that will keep you on the same path you have already picked but will show that you are not just giving up. Keep in mind these questions are hypothetical.

The decisions you make should always first prioritize saving life, then keeping the situation from escalating, minimizing the damage, and finally, preserving the scenes and evidence. This is known as the Life Safety Order and must be used to help justify which path you have chosen during Situational Questions.

Follow these rules when answering Situational Questions:

Rule: Pick a path and stick to it; stick to your guns

Rule: Use the Life Safety Order to justify your answer.

Rule: Risk a lot to save a lot and risk a little to save a little (or what is already lost).

Rule: Try to give them another option. This demonstrates critical thinking skills.

Rule: Be confident in your answer. The board will be tougher on you if you are unsure.

Let's take a look at a few examples:

Situational Question: "You just arrived at a house that is 75 percent involved in fire. From your training, you know the house is going to collapse. Are you going to go in?"

If you choose to stay out of a burning building you know is going to collapse, you should use the life safety order to justify why.

Path #1:

Response: "I am not going into a house that is going to collapse because it is my safety first, my crew second, civilians third, and property fourth."

Board: "You look inside, and you see a woman trapped under a couch. Are you going in now?"

They are trying to get you to change your answer! DON'T! Remember, stick to your guns.

Response: "I still have to say that I would not go in, but I would not give up. I would try to reach her with a pike pole or possibly a throw bag."

Again, stick to your guns. This is a horrible situation, but with the limited information given to you and the fact that it is make-believe, you need to stick to the path you chose. They will ask again to see if you will change your mind.

Board: You are unsuccessful with the throw bag and pike pole. Are you going in now?

Response: Unfortunately, I still have to say no. I did not cause the problem, but I will do everything within my power to help without risking my life. I need to think of how many lives I could save in the future. If I die here trying to save one life that is possibly already past saving, how many people could potentially die in the future? In addition, how many firefighters might get hurt or lose their lives trying to save me?

During these compounding Situational Questions, sometimes it is better to step back and look at the whole picture. If you were to go in and the building collapsed on you, you did nothing to help the situation, and, in fact, made it worse. Other firefighters might lose their lives for you. If you died in this building trying to save something that was most likely already lost, what good have you done? Think of the lives you could save in the future if you were smart and looked at the whole picture.

Now let's look at the second path you could take.

> Situational Question: You just arrived at a house that is 75 percent involved in fire. With your training, you know the house is going to collapse. Are you going to go in?

Path #2:

> Response: I would make sure I heard the orders correctly and that my captain recognized the same dangers that I did. I am a new firefighter, so it might look a lot worse to me than it actually is. I am charged with my crew's safety. I would go in with my experienced captain if he or she felt it safe. I am equipped with top-of-the-line personal protective equipment, and we have a Rapid Intervention Team in place. As long as we perform and operate within the department's Standard Operating Guidelines, I would go in.

> Board: You know the building will fall on you, are you still going in?

> Response: In this department, we are a team. I am going to be there for my captain if it did collapse. One of us would be able to drag the other out. I feel safe because all the necessary safeguards are in place. If too much time is spent deciding what to do, lives could be lost. Everything up until now has shown me that this captain to be level-headed and a great leader so I would go into any building he ordered me.

We, the co-authors, have different opinions on which path we would choose. The bottom line is that it does not matter! Pick a path, stick to the path and justify why you chose that path. Choose the one you feel confident you can defend.

Let's try another situational scenario.

Situational Question 2: You are inside a building fighting a fire and running low on air. Your captain tells you to get two new air bottles. On your way to the engine, the Battalion Chief tells you to ladder the alpha-bravo corner of the building. What are you going to do?

Path #1:

Response: I would let the Chief know that I am on an assignment to bring an air bottle to my captain. I am going to bring my captain air. I know my priority is my safety first and my crew's safety second.

Board: You are going to disregard the direct order from a Battalion Chief who has 30 years of experience?

Response: My priority is my safety first and my crew's second. I would go and get air for my captain and make sure he was safe. With my captain safe, we could both go to ladder the building. With two of us, it might even be faster and safer than trying it by myself.

The board will most likely come back with another reason why you should choose the other path. **Don't!** Remember it is a game; if you switch you lose. Remember the board has played this game many times before, and they are good at it. They will make the other path sound appealing, but you must stick to your guns.

Path #2:

Response: I would let the Chief know that I am on assignment to bring an air bottle to my captain. If the Chief still wanted me to ladder the building, I would ladder the building. I would radio my Captain to let him know I was on another assignment, and that I would be delayed getting him an air bottle.

Board: The radios are not working. Your Captain will not get the info.

Response: I would still ladder the building.

Board: You would leave your captain in there with low air?

Response: My captain is not trapped. The Battalion Chief has a lot of experience, is in charge of the entire scene, and knows my previous assignment. If he still feels that laddering the building is more important, that is what I would do.

Steer the answer:
> There might be a truck company in danger of a roof collapse or some trapped civilians that need help.

Here again they will probably come back with something to compound the situation. Just stick to your path.

D: Interpersonal Questions

We use interpersonal skills every day while dealing with people. You may know them as social skills, people skills, or emotional intelligence. The interview board considers interpersonal skills paramount when it comes to evaluating candidates. Someone with poor interpersonal skills could throw off an entire station and cause unnecessary conflict. People who have great interpersonal skills naturally get along with others and can usually empathize with those going through stressful situations. They generally thrive in a team atmosphere and possess effective communication skills with other employees and citizens. It is important to maintain and grow these skills to build trust and integrity.

Firefighters spend a great deal of time with each other under some extremely stressful situations. You will most likely be working 24-48 hours at a time with the team, so being able to get along and resolve conflicts at the lowest level possible is paramount.

Your responses to interpersonal questions give the interview board an opportunity to judge your ability to deal with conflict. You need to obtain a viable solution for all parties involved at the lowest supervisory level possible.

Rule: Try to solve at the lowest level possible. If it does not get solved, then move up the chain of command.

> **Rule: Get all the information before addressing the problem.**
>
> Interpersonal Question Example: You noticed a senior firefighter has not been completing his assigned chores, leaving you more work to accomplish on a continuous basis. This is frustrating since his apparent lazy attitude is adding significantly to your workload. How would you handle this situation?

To address interpersonal conflicts, start at the source. In the example above, you should speak directly and professionally to the senior firefighter, express your concerns, and ask if there is a reason why he has not been able to get the chores done. Perhaps the senior firefighter is having difficulties in his personal life and small details such as housework are being forgotten. The first thing you need to find out is if there is really a problem, or if you are the one who is mistaken. There would be no need to create a confrontation if you simply looked at the housework list wrong, or if there was another list you did not see.

Be cognizant of your word selection, ensuring a positive outlook. For example, you should use the word "discuss," instead of "confront." You are attempting to convey to the interview board that you are assuming the positive; using a harsh or condemning word such as confront will negate your positive outlook.

Now, think about the respect you'll earn if you address the problem privately and professionally (especially if there is an acceptable reason for the neglect), and the esteem you would lose if you handled a simple situation poorly. Remember, the last thing a busy captain wants to hear is a complaint about somebody not taking out the trash, so aim to resolve it at the lowest level!

A word of caution:

As with Situational Questions, if the interview board offers enough information to prove your fellow firefighter is blatantly disregarding his duties, you must pursue the issue up the chain of command. If the issue is unethical or poses a threat to any person's safety, this must be pursued up the chain of command, no matter how high you need to take it.

E: Bizarre, Weird, or Just Different Questions

Examples of bizarre questions taken from staffsolutions.biz "Top 20 Crazy Interview Questions by U.S.'s Greatest Companies:

How many cows are there in Canada? - Google Interview

If you were a pizza delivery person, how would you benefit from a pair of scissors? - Apple Interview

These types of questions have become popular in interviews by various large non-fire companies, but I have also heard of them being used by some Fire Departments during oral interviews. From the research we have completed, there is no right or wrong answer. The objective of these types of questions is to see how creative you are. Try to come up with something creative while incorporating the TopScore Top5.

The bottom line: **Get creative and market yourself.**

There are a variety of examples of these types of questions throughout the Internet; start coming up with some answers in your head so you are prepared to answer peculiar questions on the spot.

Follow the structure in the Real Questions chapter for the question, "What is your favorite color?"

Chapter 5 Review
Putting it into Practice

Consider the following to review the content presented in Chapter 5.

1) Use 3x5 cards and create Leading, Situational, Interpersonal, and "Weird" Questions. Mix the cards up and have a colleague or family member randomly pull cards and ask questions. Remember to:
   a. Defuse any bombs.
   b. Stay positive.
   c. Do not make pessimistic assumptions.
   d. Steer the interviewer where you want to go.
   e. List and have evidence for Interpersonal Skills.
   f. Gather all information before addressing the situation and your actions.
   g. Try to solve any conflicts presented at lowest level possible.
   h. Stay consistent on any serious ethical dilemmas that are presented.

Chapter 6
Core Values, Skills, and Abilities

In this chapter you'll learn:
- A. Core Values
- B. Skill and Abilities
    1. Interpersonal Skills
    2. Leadership
    3. Teamwork
    4. Communication Skills
    5. Professional Development
    6. Physical and Technical Expertise
    7. Innovations
    8. Diversity
    9. Customer Service

Rules: This chapter includes one Rule to help you successfully apply topics A-B listed above.

A: Overview: Core Values

Core Values are your fundamental beliefs; the underlying reason you make the decisions you make. The interview board uses your interview to determine if your Core Values line up with the department. Make their job easy by showing them what drives, motivates, and defines you.

Although you already have Core Values in place, you may not be able to identify them without forethought. Knowing and defining your Core Values will help you construct answers that will reveal them, and how they will contribute to your department.

Communicate your Core Values through action. Remember that talk is cheap, and interviewers prefer that you relay a story that reveals your application of a Core Value, rather than just listing terms.

Example: After consideration, you identify dedication as a Core Value. Rather than simply telling the board that you remain dedicated to a goal, choose Personal Stories—such as continuing to pursue the Fire Department after several failed attempts—that display dedication.

Other Core Values to consider:
- Trust
- Honesty
- Pride
- Bravery
- Persistence ✓
- Loyalty
- Honor
- Respect ✓
- Positivity
- Responsibility
- Professionalism ✓
- Self-discipline
- Initiative ✓
- Work ethic ✓
- Responsibility for your actions
- Holding true to your word

Reading this list, you may think, "I value all of those." Great. To be a good firefighter, you must. However, pick a few that truly guide your decision-making. To determine your own Core Values, ask yourself these questions:

- Which Core Values will you make sacrifices for in order to maintain?
- Which ones do you see throughout your entire life?
- At the end of your life, what characteristics will your friends and family use to describe you?

Rule: Develop stories the board will remember.

B: Skill and Abilities

In addition to holding positive Core Values, successful firefighters must exhibit specific skills. No firefighter—past or present—has fully mastered any of these skills. You won't either. The board looks for candidates who have made it a point to develop these skills in the past and who will continue to in the future.

Do not consider this an exhaustive list. Yours can be different, but keep these in mind:

1. Interpersonal Skills

I recently attended a family friend's 50th anniversary party. After the party ended, I offered to assist with cleaning up the plates and cups, as well as vacuuming the floors and putting away the tables and chairs. I volunteered under the direction of an 80-year-old man who was the type of person that wanted things done according to his particular process for clearing tables and putting the table and chairs away. Though it was clear there was a more efficient method, out of respect and patience, I followed his lead. Sure, it may have taken 10 minutes longer than how I would have done it, but I was aware that he needed followers more than I wanted to fulfill my natural desire to lead. This would be an example of interpersonal skills.

You are with the same people for as much as 48 hours at a time when on duty at the firehouse. There will be times when your co-workers will get on your nerves. If your children (who you care so much about) can get under your skin, imagine how a middle-aged individual who snores and passes copious amounts of bodily gasses (and to whom you have no physical relation) could set you off! You must display interpersonal skills on a daily basis, not just when on a call.

If you feel your Interpersonal Skills are lacking, we recommend reading books or watching videos on emotional intelligence. You can easily start by finding several TED Talks on YouTube to help expand your understanding of emotional intelligence and improve your skills.

GROUNDWORK:

Think of five times you displayed positive interpersonal skills and write them down. Trust us, you have them, even if you are a high school graduate who is just beginning to enter the workforce.

1. Inter-departmental teams (website)
2. Training of new employees @ CoR
3. Working w/ sub-contractors on House project
4. Daily work interpreting & enforcing Codes
5.

2. Leadership

Leadership is the ability to positively influence others toward the achievement of a goal. Leaders exude self-confidence (not arrogance) and respect the thoughts and opinions of others. Strong leadership fosters teamwork that creates an atmosphere that inspires others to achieve their full potential. Outstanding leaders have a vision of excellence that motivates and provides encouragement. A leader's demonstrated integrity creates a level of trust and confidence. Leading by example is the expectation of all firefighters, especially when interacting with the community.

At some point in time, every excellent leader has needed to follow someone else's direction. It is no different in the fire service. Everyone must answer to someone in a position above himself or herself. The firefighter answers to the Captain, the Captain to the Battalion Chief (BC), the BC to the Fire Chief, the Fire Chief to the Mayor, and so on.

From the first day as a probationary rookie, you must learn to be a good follower. You'll need to follow Standard Operating Procedures, employee handbooks, and direct instructions from your training captain and then from your crew. It is important to show the board how you have been successful as a follower in previous jobs and life experiences while simultaneously expressing to the board your previous and current ability to lead.

Think about where and when you have displayed positive leadership skills, and write a list of five times you have displayed unique leadership skills.

GROUNDWORK:

How I've Demonstrated Leadership:

1. DSC leader on website
2. Lead my group on innovative permit processing
3. Organized Recreational Soccer/Trail running
4. led extra-curricular groups in college
5. Volunteer for special assignments @ work

3. Teamwork

Every highly functioning Fire Department operates as a team. The success of each call and the safety of you, your team, and the community hinges on teamwork.

If you're not already, you should participate actively on a team or committee. Build respect from peers by contributing to the goals of the group. Model expected behaviors to accomplish team goals. Commit to the success of the group. Focus on the group's needs when taking actions. Act professionally and demonstrate flexibility. Always consider the impact of your actions on the group.

Everyone, and we mean everyone, has been part of a team. Teamwork should be one of the strongest points you will display. Think about where and when you have exhibited outstanding teamwork in your own life and write a list of five times you have displayed it.

GROUNDWORK:

Ways I've Demonstrated Teamwork:

1. Team Soccer @ High level
2. Work on various special projects @ work
3. Crossfit & competitions
4. Construction Project manager
5. Various team projects @ college. City presentations

4. Communication Skills

All professional positions require excellent communication skills. Nearly every applicant for any position will highlight his or her strong communication skills, but only a few possess the type of communication skills the board is seeking.

Excellent communication skills require highly developed listening skills, as well as verbal, nonverbal (body language), and writing skills. You should listen actively and engage the person with whom you are communicating.

Convince the board of your strong communication skills by evidencing them during your interview. From the moment you walk in the door you need to be fully engaged; remember their names, listen to all parts of the questions, never interrupt, speak and conduct yourself with confidence, be clear, and avoid rambling. The board will use this single interaction with you to determine if they trust you to communicate well with your team, the community, and your superiors.

When most people share their ability to communicate, they default to thinking of times when they were able to effectively communicate the point they wanted to make. For me, one of the toughest communication components can be listening, and more importantly, listening to my shortcomings. I remember one of my first jobs as a young teen working with a few friends on a landscape crew. It was a job outside under the sun, and I was getting paid to hang out and visit with my friends who were also on the landscape crew. After two weeks on the job, I was called into the boss's office for my first evaluation. I walked into the meeting expecting a good report. I showed up to work early, worked as hard as or harder than most, and never complained. He let me know the things I did well, which were music to my ears. He then said if I wanted to stay employed with him that I needed to eliminate the horsing around I did with my friends while on the clock. He also said that as a newer hire to the company, I needed to talk less and listen more. I remember saying to him that I would work on those things, but felt the pain of what I initially accepted as an insult.

It was tough stuff to hear as a 16-year-old, but he was right. Sometimes being a good listener can be tough, especially if you feel you are getting your backend chewed. The bottom line, however, was that I was better for it. Listening has become a new priority for me whenever I am coached by someone who speaks of my shortcomings.

GROUNDWORK:

Write a list of five times you have showcased your communication skills.

1. Daily work @ COR - Explain complicated processes - work across the counter
2.
3.
4.
5.

5. Professional Development

Until the day you retire, you should pursue your job, advance your skills, and always be learning. Every year, new research comes out that must be implemented to ensure the best practices possible. A stale firefighter puts lives at risk every day. The board will only offer the job to you if they believe you will continue to grow your entire career. Convince them by showing how you have done this in the past and what your goals are in the future.

Professional development is continuous and is achieved in a variety of ways: continuing education, seminars and podcasts, on the job experience, and learning from and sharing with other firefighters.

GROUNDWORK:

Write a list of five ways you have pursued professional development.

1. PT, IRC, IBC
2. Remodel house to gain knowledge hands on
3. P.T. to P.E.
4. Continuing Ed & Classes on codes
5.

6. Physical and Technical Expertise

As a firefighter, you are required to be in great shape with a high level of cardiovascular fitness. Some Fire Departments require a mile-and-a-half run in less than 11 minutes, 30 seconds or employ other physical agility tests as part of entry-level testing. Begin a fitness program today. Your physical presence makes a strong impression to the oral board when you walk through the door. You need to show the board that not only you are fit for duty now, but that you will be fit for duty 25 years from now. No Fire Department wants to invest in a candidate not willing to commit to the level of fitness the fire service requires. Start now!

GROUNDWORK:

Write a list of five ways you maintain an active lifestyle and stay physically fit.

1. Trail run, completions
2. Crossfit
3. Soccer
4. Hiking & camping
5.

7. Innovation

Firefighters never go on the exact same call twice. Therefore, we can't predict or practice every call; however, we must be prepared for every situation. This requires innovation!

Innovators are not afraid of change and are willing to consider a variety of alternative solutions. They possess the vision of where they would like to go and explore multiple options allowing them to reach their desired destinations. At the same time, innovators understand the various impacts of change and strive to think through options and consequences carefully before acting.

GROUNDWORK:

Write a list of five times you have displayed innovation.

1. Record keeping Procedures
2. Software enhancements
3. LEAN Processes @ work
4.
5.

8. Diversity

Both the Fire Department and the community you serve as a firefighter are diverse. In order to do your job well, you must understand and value the contributions made by persons of all nationalities, races, colors, sexual orientations, and political and religious ideologies.

Diversity reaches beyond the categories protected by law and includes the differences that make us unique as human beings. You must be confident enough in your own beliefs to appreciate a different perspective or point of view.

GROUNDWORK:

Write a list of five times you have embraced diversity in your own life.

1.
2.
3.
4.
5.

9. Customer Service Skills

Have you ever thought of the fire service as part of the customer service industry? It is. Firefighters with excellent customer service skills strive to ensure every person they have contact with, whether on or off a call, be treated with respect. It is important to realize the needs of the customer take precedence over the needs of the person delivering the service. You must understand and accept that perception is just as important as the service delivered.

An example good of Customer Service:

I worked for a local grocery store during high school, and my employer prided himself on the store's high level of superior customer service. On the first page of the employee handbook, I remember reading a particular paragraph that stated, "If it is good for the customer and falls in line with the Core Values of the store, then it is a win-win."

One night, I was helping an elderly woman and bagging her groceries. With the task completed, I asked her if I could take them out to her car. She replied that she lived behind the store in the mobile home park and planned to make a few trips walking back and forth using a cart she left by the front door of her house. I told her I wasn't going to let that happen, and walked her cart and groceries to her front door. This was a specific incident not covered in the handbook, other than the broad statement listed above. I did follow up through the chain of command to my immediate supervisor, and he was pleased with the decision and said he would support that type of customer service any day.

GROUNDWORK:

Think about where and when you have exhibited superb customer service skills in your own life and write a list of five times you have displayed these traits.

1.
2.
3.
4.
5.

Chapter 6 Review
Putting it Into Play

Consider the following to review the content presented in Chapter 6.

1) Create a Venn Diagram in order to discover which personal Core Values best align with the Core Values of your target department.

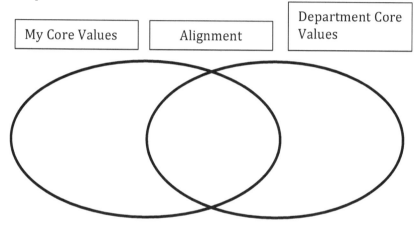

2) On a separate piece of paper, draw and complete the following organizer for each Core Value to ensure that you have evidence of each value in action. Recall stories and examples to illustrate your Core Value.

Story/Example 1: How is this value displayed in my personal life?		Story/Example 3: How is this value displayed in my personal life?
	My Core Value Defined	
Story/Example 2: How is this value displayed in my personal life?		Story/Example 4: How is this value displayed in my personal life?

Chapter 7
Marketing Priorities

In this chapter you'll learn:
- A. Overview: Marketing Priorities
- B. Example Marketing Priorities
- C. Marketing Priorities Blended into TopScore Answer

Rules: This chapter includes two Rules to help you successfully apply topics A-C listed above.

A: TopScore Marketing Priorities

When you become confident in the interview game, you can start to tailor your answers to align with the greatest needs of the department you are interviewing with. These needs become your Marketing Priorities. If the department takes pride in their members' level of fitness, then you, as a fit person, might have fitness as one of the Marketing Priorities to communicate in your interview. This means your Marketing Priorities change depending on the department.

Marketing Priorities are simply your top skills, values, and experience that set you up for the specific department.

Your Marketing Priorities can be made up of components of your TopScore Top5. Some of the items you listed in your Personal History, Personal Story, or Core Values may overlap into your Marketing Priorities. When they do overlap, you should be committed to sharing those items before you leave the interview.

If you have past firefighting experience, it will become your number one Marketing Priority. Show the board that you have successfully filled the role and remain passionate about it. When highlighting your past experience, make sure you do not come across as arrogant but rather as teachable.

If you don't have past fire experience, don't be discouraged as departments continuously hire candidates without fire experience. Most departments would rather hire someone passionate about the job than someone who has experience but lacks excitement. The board can predict what type of success you will have by evaluating your non-fire background and applying the skills toward firefighting.

For example, the board may find an accountant who is an outdoor enthusiast with a high level of fitness, intelligence, and loves working with people more admirable than a five-year volunteer firefighter who comes in and shows no excitement. If you fall into this rookie category, you should look at other experiences/skills that align with the skills needed to be a successful firefighter. Study the department's job description so you can determine how to align yourself perfectly with it. Not every question will lend itself to sharing a Marketing Priority.

Rule: Make sure you have perfected the TopScore Top5 before you start adding the Marketing Priorities.

Rule: Blend your Marketing Priorities with the TopScore Top5 for the best possible answer.

B: Example Marketing Priorities

Notice how Rob's 10 Marketing Priorities prior to getting hired as a firefighter overlap with the TopScore Top5:

1) Hotshot Crew Member. I worked for one of the United States' premier Hotshot wild land firefighting crews. The team worked in extremely hazardous environments, both physically and mentally arduous. We were expected to be in peak physical fitness at all times because we worked for days straight without sleep. This was my first real test with working in stressful conditions, and I was successful.
2) My values include being honest, being a man of integrity, and exhibiting a great work ethic. The same ideals that this department is seeking in a new hire are the same ideals my parents raised me with since birth. My parents have always taught me the importance of respecting others as well as respecting myself, which has helped me fulfill my potential.

3) My high level of superior customer service. The fire service is in the business of providing customer service to its taxpayers. I was named Courtesy Clerk of the year in 1990, predominantly because of the level of customer service I demonstrated.
4) I am a dedicated teammate. Sports have been part of my life since I was 6 years old. I have played on teams that went undefeated as well as those who didn't win a single game. My memories of the years in which we finished last are not morose and regretful, but memories of the fun we all had playing together.
5) Dependable. I have always been described as being dependable. I think it goes back to what I was taught growing up regarding giving someone my word and sticking to it. If there is something that needs to be done, I am your man.
6) I take pride in my work. I perform exceptional work and sign my name to it. I am not the kind of person who sacrifices speed for a shabby job.
7) Volunteer work. I enjoy volunteer work. One of my favorite jobs was volunteering during the winter at a local hospital where I answered phones and assisted with delivering flowers and balloons from the gift shop.
8) I am adaptable to any given changing situation. I grew up in a broken household. My parents divorced when I was 10, and this started a windfall of change. At age 14, I moved from California, where I was living with my mom, to Boise to live with my father. I had lived in the same town with my same friend my entire life, but despite that, I was able to meet and make friends almost immediately. I adapted to the changing situation, and moreover, I thrived.
9) My physical abilities. Being a firefighter requires a high level of both strength and cardio. I lift weights three days a week and either run or mountain bike the other days.
10) I am already a student of the trade. It is my ambition to be an exceptional, professional firefighter. My desire and passion have me reading numerous firefighting publications and learning as much as I can. My brother, who is also a firefighter, shared that a firefighter will always be learning about the trade until his last day on the job.

C: Marketing Priorities Blended into TopScore

When practicing your interview, work on blending your Marketing Priorities (MP) and Core Values (CV) together; we refer to those components as the polish. The blending must be practiced so your responses sound natural and fluent rather than coerced and rehearsed. Here is an example of a polished answer to one of the most common Real Questions:

Oral board: Tell us about yourself.

Response: My Name is Fred Gibbons. I grew up in a family of **(PH)** five on a **(PH)** tree farm where I learned **(Core Value, CV)(KW)** work ethic, **(KW)(CV)** personal values, and the **(CV)** importance of supporting those around you, just like you do here in the fire service. **(PS)** Some of my fondest childhood memories include my dad taking me by **(DK)** Station 1 and letting me climb on the trucks in my plastic firefighter helmet. As is **(KW)** tradition in the fire service and Backdraft Fire, **(DK)** the doors were always open, and my questions were answered with enthusiasm.

I am currently a **(Marketing Priority, MP)(PH)** paid reserve firefighter for a local Fire Department. I have earned both **(MP)(PH)** FF1 and **(MP)(PH)** EMT with them. I've always taken a personal interest in **(KW)** physical fitness. I'm an avid **(PH)** mountain biker, **(PH)** runner and rock climber, and I participated in **(PH)** high school sports. **(MP)** I have participated in multiple fundraiser **(PH)** stair climbs and a **(PH)** mountain bike race series in Oregon. I bring these up because it's an example of who I am and the lifestyle I live. These events allow me to stay **(KW)(MP)** active and involved with my **(KW)** community. I know how important volunteering is within the community. I have traveled and **(KW)** volunteered in some very **(KW)(MP)** diverse cultures. I also understand the **(DK)** importance of **(PH)** physical fitness and **(KW)(CV)** diversity to Backdraft Fire. I've had opportunities to speak with department members, and I understand the **(KW)** high physical standards —including running, push-ups, and sit-ups **(DK)** — expected during the **(DK)** recruit academy and throughout my career. **(DK)** I've seen Backdraft Firefighters' participation in the Seattle Stair Climb and other local events.

Additionally, I am not **(PH)** married. I have two kids, one chocolate lab and one black lab. I currently work in the **(PH)** construction field as a **(PH)** framer, and at this time, I have yet to hammer a finger. I am very excited about this great opportunity to be interviewing with such a **(KW)** progressive Fire Department.

GROUNDWORK:

For your Marketing Priorities, make a list of your top 25 attributes. These can be anything from a great sense of humor to a fierce loyalty to friends and family. This may seem like a large number, so brainstorm. Remember, there are no wrong ideas when you are brainstorming. Ask family and friends to assist you in this endeavor. Look at your Personal History from above. Examples might include your education, work history, and awards. Some of these may even be obvious and listed on your résumé. For example, maybe you worked as a wild land firefighter. This crucial piece of information needs to be presented to the oral board. Remember: brainstorm! Your past needs to come out!

Once you have 25 items on your list, narrow it down to 10. Once again, use those closest to you to assist you in paring down the 25 to your top 10. Ask yourself where do the needs of the department and firefighting overlap with your Personal History, Personal Story, and skills. Then rank in importance using basic common sense. Which one most supports your candidacy for the position?

These 10 stories are your TopScore Marketing Priorities. They will be molded with the Core Value answers you formed previously and crafted into an answer using the TopScore Top5 structure. It will take practice, but once mastered, you will speak flawlessly when sitting before the oral panel.

Chapter 7 Review
Putting it into Play

Consider the following to review the content presented in Chapter 7.

In collaboration with those who know you best, brainstorm and list 20 of your Marketing Priorities.

1) On the same piece of paper, cross out half so you are left with 10 of your strongest and most evident Marketing Priorities.
2) On a separate sheet of paper, identify the greatest needs of your target department.
3) Align your Marketing Priorities to the needs of the target department.
4) Your result can look something like this:

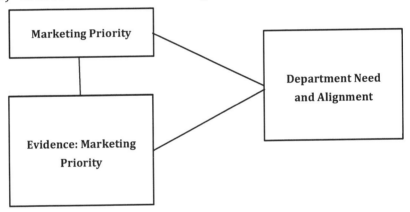

Chapter 8
Oral Interview Wrap Up

In this chapter you'll learn:

A. Closing Remarks
B. Thank You Card
C. Additional TopScore Rules
D. Sample Interview Questions
E. Sample "What If" Questions

Rules: This chapter includes 26 Rules to help you successfully apply topics A-E listed above.

A: Closing Remarks

Be thoroughly prepared for the board to close with a question such as "Is there anything you would like to add?" Look at it as an opportunity to let the board know about one or two of your Marketing Priorities that you might have missed. As a fellow interviewer stated, "I have never given a perfect score to an interviewee if this question was not answered." This is a valuable opportunity; use it to your advantage!

During your closing remarks, you should briefly touch on each of the following items. Don't delve too deeply into these items. Your response should be a concise summary of what you have discussed during the interview:

- Summarize your qualifications.
- Emphasize one of your best 10 Marketing Priorities.
- Reiterate how you would fit the department's values.
- Illustrate how proud you will be to be a part of the department.
- Thank them for their time and inform them you look forward to working with them in the future.

B: Thank You Card

Rule: Write a thank you card.

A thank you card is one last opportunity to positively influence the interview board. To date, you've provided a professional résumé and excelled at the interview. The interview board will take a copy of your résumé to assist them while they determine the rank-order of the entire interview pool. Think of the thank you card as an opportunity to reiterate your name, and show how interested you are in becoming a member of their department.

Rule: Handwrite the thank you card.

Rule: Address them by name and rank. (e.g. Captain Rogers)

A handwritten card demonstrates a desire to go beyond what the average candidate would do. Let's face it; not many people handwrite letters these days. Anybody can sit down for a few seconds and fire off a clean-looking email with the use of grammar and spell check, but few are willing to take the time to handwrite a thank you card to each of the board members. Ensure that you mail them in time for the interviewers to receive soon after the interview. Write the cards immediately after the interview and mail them either the same day or the following day at the latest.

DO NOT use this as an opportunity to remind the board members of why you would be a great hire. Your successful interview already answered that question.

C: Additional TopScore Rules for the Oral Interview

What may be apparent to some is not apparent to all. These simple rules will enable you to make a positive first impression on the oral board and gain their interest from the moment you walk into the room. Fail to follow these rules and you will significantly decrease your chances of gaining your badge before the interview has even begun. Some of these rules may be found elsewhere in this book; it might be because they are important!

Rule: Social media. There are many different types of background checks that Fire Departments conduct. Make sure your social media accounts are not offensive in any way.

Rule: Prepare for a background investigation. Get all your background items collected before you need them. Some background checks are 15 pages of information. You will only have one week to collect everything. If you have moved out of state from where you went to high school and college, this will make it difficult to acquire your transcripts in time. Do the work beforehand. This info will also be helpful in filling out your application. Some background checks can go back 10 years or more.

Rule: Application. Get your application in first. Have someone proofread it, even if you are an English major and the world spelling bee champion four years in a row.

Rule: Résumé. Get it done right the first time. There are classes or software if you do not want to pay a professional. Keep the résumé to one page. We are professionals, but you are not applying to be the CEO of a major corporation.

Rule: Show up 30 minutes early for your interview. If they are ahead of schedule, your effort will be noticed and appreciated.

Rule: Leave your cell phone in your car. Even if you have all the information you are trying to remember on your phone, it will look like you are posting on the internet.

Rule: Be enthusiastic. Nobody wants to spend 30 minutes listening to a humdrum, monotone voice. Have some enthusiasm and engage them.

Rule: Smile as often as you can during the interview. Smiling is contagious and makes people feel good. When you smile, it also shows the board that you are enjoying yourself despite the stress of the interview.

Rule: Dress to impress. This is a job of professionals. You need to dress as such.

Rule: Handshake. Your handshake must be firm but not overpowering.

Rule: Body language. Your body language accounts for an enormous amount of what you communicate. Be engaging. Recording your Mock Interviews allows you to assess your body language and correct any issues. Take a neutral body position. Sit as if a string were connecting your head to the ceiling. Leaning back or slouching in the chair is seen as lazy or arrogant and leaning forward can be perceived as overly aggressive.

Rule: Eye contact. Strong eye contact shows confidence, and confidence is a sign of leadership. Eye contact should be made with each person on the oral board while you speak. Eye contact starts with the person who asks the question and from there, make eye contact with everyone else on the board, even if someone is ignoring you. Your answer should finish with eye contact with the person who initiated the question.

Rule: Be confident, not arrogant. I have heard of people not being hired because they came across as too arrogant.

Rule: The chair. If your chair is 20 feet or more away from the board, ask if you can move it up. They will probably say, "Sure." Move it up to where you are closer, but don't lean on or touch the table.

Rule: Lose the "ums." If they are counting your ums, you will probably not get hired. If you set the record, you definitely won't get hired! Record your Mock Interviews, count the number of times you use filler language like "um," and strive to eliminate them.

Rule: "The Ignore." One of the oral board members will not look at you. Ever! You must still try to make eye contact and try to engage him, as this is part of the test.

Rule: Positive statements. If the oral board asks how you feel working with different types of people, ensure them you only think positively and answer accordingly.

Rule: Never lie. Don't lie or try to get one over on these guys. They are on the board because they are very good judges of character.

Rule: Do not chew gum. This should go without saying, but it would not be here unless someone had done it.

Rule: Do not interrupt anyone.

Rule: Never include the following statements in your interview answer:

"The 20 days off a month will be great for me to have a second job."

"I am simply looking for a career change."

"I hope to get a few years of experience, so I can go back to my home city and test."

"I am getting bored in my current job."

D: Sample Questions

Use the following sample questions to practice. Some might seem strange, but you need to find a way to relate them to the fire service using the TopScore Top5 system.

Who is your favorite past president of the U.S. and why?

This is a perfect answer to incorporate Keywords. Pick five good Keywords and match them with a president.

What is the most important inventions of all time and why?

Use this one to demonstrate your Department Knowledge. Pick an invention and relate it to what you know about the department. Take, for example, the wheel. Talk about how the department benefits from the invention of the wheel and transition to your Department Knowledge. You can start with the facts that there are six wheels on each apparatus. They have 20 engines, six trucks, and a maintenance division to maintain the apparatus. Wheels are needed to respond to 30,000 calls per year with a ratio of 75 percent medical, 10 percent fire, and 15 percent miscellaneous responses.

Why is it important to be dependable?

Dependability is contagious; it shows dedication and it carries over. Dependability makes people passionate about working hard for each other. It can be contagious within an organization. Being dependable fosters trust in your teammates, community, and supervisors while illustrating your dedication to obtain a goal and the self-sacrifice to get there.

What word would best describe you?

Look at the department's mission statement and Core Values to formulate this answer.

What is the most appealing aspect of being a firefighter?

You will need to figure this out on your own. Do not say anything like it will give me a lot of time to have a second job.

How could you help maintain good relationships around the firehouse?

Be nice and show interest in your fellow firefighters' families and hobbies.

What are three characteristics of a good firefighter?

Look at the department's mission statement and Core Values; let them know which ones you have.

What type of person would you find most difficult to work with?

Think of safety when answering this question.

Define honesty and integrity and tell why they are important in the fire service.

What do you think about unions?

A union representative will likely be on your interview board! Talk to him. Look at the history of unions and why they started.

What do you know about the organizational structure of the department?

Know that most departments have the following divisions: Administration Division, Operations Division, Training Division, Prevention Division, and Logistics Division.

Give some examples of how you provide customer service in your current job.

What is the primary goal of the Fire Department?

Think of customer service.

What do you think of your previous boss?

Answer with only positive statements.

What motivates you?

Think of your Keywords.

Give an example of when you worked with someone different than you.

Again, use only positive language.

Would you ever disobey an order?

Yes, if it has to do with my safety or the safety of others.

Define sexual harassment and give your feelings about the subject.

Think about this before your interview.

What have you done to prepare for this position?

I like to think that everything I have done in life so far has helped me prepare for this position.

What are you bringing to the job?

Why should we select you over other candidates?

This is a good question for using Department Knowledge and Keywords.

Why do you want to work for this agency?

What do you know about this agency?

What are your strengths?

Find out what their department values are and tailor your answers. They could include customer service, fitness, tradition, and many other things.

What are your weaknesses?

Have a weakness that will not keep you from being hired, but you can show that you are working on and it is getting better. Do not have a weakness that is really a strength; the oral board will see right through it.

What would your employer say about you?

Have you ever been in an emergency situation?

What is the least appealing aspect of being a firefighter?

Taking the firefighter oath will require you to experience things you don't even want to imagine. This question is more concerned with what you care about; missing holidays with your family, working a 24 or 48-hour shift, or the extremely challenging and heartbreaking calls you will face. You can add a positive take to your response by acknowledging the department's quality training and your ability to cope with difficult situations and willingness to seek support when needed.

What do you think the future holds for the fire service?

Are you currently on any other eligibility lists?

What is the primary goal of the Fire Department?

Talk about the history of Fire Departments, as well as why and who developed the fire service.

When and how did you fail in a job or assignment?

What makes you think that you will be able to deal with the stress and strains of the job?

How do you and your family feel about working 24-hour shifts?

What is the advantage of working in teams?

What is the disadvantage of working in teams?

How do you handle conflict?

Describe a time when you disagreed with a coworker.

Describe a time you were asked to do something wrong.

What is the toughest decision you have ever had to make?

What does leadership mean to you?

Give examples.

Why is a healthy lifestyle important to the fire service?

What does integrity mean to you? How do you practice it?

What is your biggest mistake in life?

How do you evaluate success?

Why are you leaving your current job?

What are the attributes of a firefighter? What is the most important to you?

What are three characteristics of a good firefighter? Which do you have?

Where do you see yourself in five years? Ten years?

Describe a difficult problem you had to overcome.

How would your friends describe you?

Who has inspired you in life?

How would you handle racist/sexist comments?

Why do you want to be a firefighter?

You would be surprised how many people do not have an answer for this question.

E: Example "What If" Questions

What if you suspect a fellow firefighter has a drug problem?

What if you see a fellow firefighter slip an expensive watch into his turnout coat during overhaul?

What if during the final exam of your probationary academy, you see two fellow recruits exchanging answers?

What if your captain orders you to get him a radio from the engine, and on the way, the Battalion Chief stops you and asks you to deliver an axe to the roof right away?

What if you feel a fellow firefighter is not pulling his or her weight?

What if you are assigned a task that you strongly feel is unsafe?

What if your shift Captain clearly delegates much more work to you than the other firefighters on the shift who happen to be his drinking buddies?

Chapter 8 Review
Putting it Into Play

Consider the following to review the content presented in Chapter 8.

Now that you are familiar with all parts of the TopScore Top5 system, use the following organizer to answer the provided Sample Questions. Remember, if it is a Real Question, use all parts; for What If Questions, use only applicable areas.

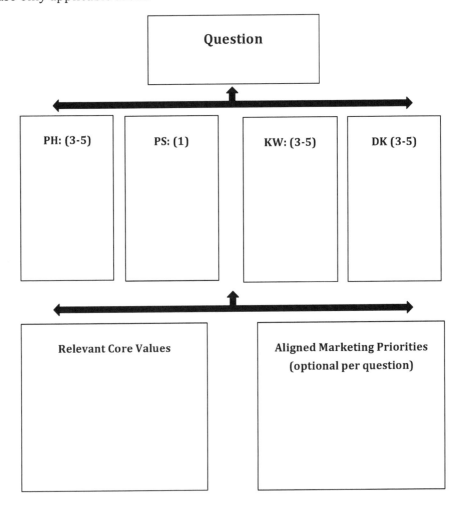

Chapter 9
Ride-along Rules

In this chapter you'll learn:
- A. About the Ride-along
- B. Ride-along Rules
- C. Ride-along Questions

Rules: This chapter includes 12 Rules to help you successfully apply the topics listed above.

A. About the Ride-along

A department ride-along is the perfect opportunity to learn about your prospective department and meet your future co-workers. It gives you the chance to make a good impression, ask important questions, and show the department that you are serious about getting hired. However, not knowing the rules and expectations could cost you the job. If you make a bad impression, you can be sure it will travel through the department before you ever get to the interview. An old adage describing the fastest ways to spread news is, "Telegraph, telephone, or tell a firefighter!"

In almost every agency, ride-alongs require filling out some paperwork that usually includes a liability waiver.

B: Ride-along Rules

Rule: Do the ride-along! If your department doesn't do ride-alongs or isn't currently accepting any, ask if you can do a station visit instead. Alternatively, you can request a ride-along with a neighboring department or cooperative team. For example, you could do a ride-along with an ambulance service or police department that regularly runs calls with the Fire Department.

Rule: Wear appropriate clothing in layers. You want to dress professionally but still be geared for a dynamic environment. Wear business casual with clean, closed-toe comfortable shoes. A collared polo shirt or button-down shirt with khaki pants is appropriate. No hats. Bring a jacket if needed for the weather.

Rule: Leave your phone in the car. If you want to take some notes, use a pen and paper.

Rule: Knock with your elbows. It has been history in the service for a probationary firefighter to bring dessert when arriving for the first time at his or her assigned station. With hands full, they had no other way to knock than with their elbows. You may not be a probie yet, but play the part. Show your appreciation by bringing a treat to share with the crew. It is not required, just recommended (even though we call it a rule).

Rule: Speak less and listen more. Your first ride-along can be very exciting, which sometimes leads to motor mouth syndrome. Talking too much can come across like you aren't interested in learning; practice asking questions and listening rather than talking. It should go without saying that profanity and other unprofessional speech has no place in this environment.

Rule: Bring your own meal(s). If you will be at the station during lunch or dinner provide your own meals. If the crew invites you to eat with them, pay your share. Sitting at the table will give you a personal and in-depth understanding of their world and their perspective, and is another good time to speak less and listen more.

Rule: Follow Instructions. Follow the instructions of both the department and the host engine or truck company officer. This is a major responsibility for the agency and the officer; it's important to respect that.

Rule: Jump in and help! When crews are sweeping floors, washing the rigs or doing dishes, get involved and lend a hand. Stay away from the recliner and the T.V. during downtime; grab a firefighting magazine or book and sit at the kitchen table and learn something.

Rule: Confidentiality. Firefighters see a lot of interesting things in their line of work. Not even Hollywood can make up what firefighters see in real life. As a participant in a ride-along, you may see neighbors and other people from your community at their worst moment. Specifics and identifiers from the call are not for public knowledge unless otherwise agreed upon. Adhere to all HIPAA regulations, as you will be held accountable to the same standards.

Rule: Thank You. Shake hands with and thank all members at the fire house.

Rule: You don't have a chance. When you go for your ride-alongs, the crews will tell you they already know who they are going to hire. Don't let it get to you; they are just trying to see if they can scare you away easily. Just show them that if it is true, they are making a mistake.

C. Ride-along Questions

Rule: Have your TopScore ride-along questions ready.

Below you'll find a list of questions you can ask during your ride-along. Don't consider this a comprehensive list; think about your own questions you have. What interests you? Show you care about the fire service and the crewmembers, not just that you want information for your interview.

The basis for the following questions was given to me (Michael Zolin) by Michael Cisneros, the Stockton Firefighter who mentored me for my first firefighter interview 20 years ago. These questions are still relevant today; however, with the internet, it is much easier to find the answers. During your interview, it is good to have information that can be found online, but it is much better to have information that can't be found online.

- Does the department have paramedics? Is there a goal to grow the paramedic program?
- What is the department's ISO rating? (insurance rating)
- Who is the Training Officer? Background?
- Number of calls?
- Call percentages? Fire/Medical/other?
- What is the fire loss per year?
- What is the department budget?
- What is the department work schedule?
- What is the training-drill frequency, and what type of activities are covered?
- What type of apparatus is located at the station?

- Is there any special equipment at the station? (e.g., Brush fire rigs or a riverboat?)
- What is the average response time?
- How many battalions are in the department?
- Are there any high-rise buildings in the district?
- What is the pre-fire plan?
- How many jobs are available?
- Are there any unique hazards to the station? (e.g., refineries, lumber yards, chemical storage, rivers, or highways)
- What specialty teams are located at the station? (e.g. Dive team or Hazmat)
- What stations are the busiest?
- What station is the best? Dog house?
- Does the department use Incident Command? Blue Card?
- What sports are played by the firefighters in the department?
- What is the department's history?
- How many recruits fail the fire academy?
- Who is the medical transport?
- How long is the academy, and what type of training can be anticipated?
- What does an average day consist of?
- For which nonprofit groups does the Union raise money?

GROUNDWORK:

1. Prepare questions
2. Schedule your ride-along

Chapter 10
Mock Interviews
and Self Score Rubrics

In this chapter you'll learn:
- A. An overview to practice
- B. Filling in your own Scoresheet
- C. TopScore Interview Scoresheet
- D. TopScore Top5 Scorecard

A: An Overview to Practice

To truly grasp and implement the concepts discussed in this book, you will need to practice and practice, and when you have done that, practice some more!

We are huge proponents of the mock oral interview. These Mock Interviews can be done with family or friends, or if you happen to know a firefighter, try to get it done at a fire station in front of firefighters. If practicing at a fire station, make sure you bring a peace offering, such as cookies or donuts, and thank them for their time. Practicing these Mock Interviews with people you are less comfortable with will help you to perform in the nerve-racking environment of the oral board. Regardless of where your Mock Interview is done, you need to wear business professional attire, just as you will for your real interview.

Make it your goal to do at least four mock oral interviews within two weeks of reading this book. This will allow you to become comfortable with the skills you've learned and hone your presentation by practicing in front of people. Use your phone to record your Mock Interview. This will provide you a frank assessment of your interview skills and allow you to identify areas in the delivery of your responses upon which you can improve.

When reviewing your Mock Interview, count each non-verbal pause. Count how many times you fill a void in the conversation with unnecessary words such as "um." Using these unnecessary filler words provides a chance for your brain to catch up with what you are trying to say. If you say "um" frequently, you need to find a way to stop. If you need a moment to gather your thoughts, take a three-second pause; the board will not interrupt you.

We recommend recording your Mock Interviews and evaluating yourself after. You will catch things your Mock Interview board won't. After doing this several times, you will also be encouraged and see improvement.

We provide two different ways to evaluate your Mock Interviews: example panel Scoresheets based on five characteristics and Scorecards designed to evaluate your use of the Topscore Top5. The next two sections will discuss both.

B: Filling in Your Own Scoresheet

Now that you understand the TopScore process and can craft quality answers, you need to understand the five categories typically used to grade a candidate. These five categories are: Leadership, Interpersonal Sensitivity, Cultural Diversity, Oral Communication, and Problem Solving and Reasoning. The TopScore Interview Scoresheet will measure how well you perform within these five categories.

To effectively practice for your interview, you need to know how the oral board will evaluate you. For example, when my (Rob) 6-year-old daughter prepares to be judged during her gymnastics competition, she understands that the judges will award her more points if her cartwheel is completed with straight legs. This item is important enough to warrant a specific block on the judge's Scoresheet. From the first day she learned a cartwheel, the importance of having straight legs was instilled in her mind, so much so that when she cartwheels around the house, she looks for feedback on the straightness of her legs.

In the same way, you need to understand what is on the interviewer's Scoresheet, and ensure you check every block for each question. You should make it effortless for the interviewer to award you the maximum score for your interview.

The Scoresheet uses a point grading system that although is somewhat subjective, the following guidelines will help you determine where you fall.

Excellent Skills   90 to 100

You have provided three or more examples that back up this claim (leadership etc.). You have displayed all aspects of the skill. Your understanding of this skill is obvious. You can talk about it confidently and understand its importance.

Good Skills   80 to 90

You have provided one to two examples with significant details that back up this claim. Your understanding of this skill is obvious; however, the skill doesn't stand out against other skills. There may be some aspects of the skill that you have not displayed but claim.

Acceptable Skills   70 to 80

You have claimed the skill several times, but your experience doesn't specifically highlight it. It seems you understand what the skill includes, but you do not convince the board that you have displayed the skill continuously in your past.

In some cases, you've said all the right things, but your delivery doesn't convince the board. For example, you claim to be a strong, confident leader and provide examples; however, your use of "ums" and lack of eye contact makes the board question your confidence.

Poor Skills   60 to 70

You do not mention the skill or share an example that displays you possess the skill, or you mention the skill but do not accurately define it or understand its importance in the Fire Department.

C: TopScore Interview Scoresheet

Leadership

Motivates others to take desired action or adopt attitudes having a positive effect on behavior; guides a group with common tasks or goals toward task/goal accomplishment; commands attention and respect, shows an air of confidence; originates action and attempts to influence events to achieve goals; sets task objectives and priorities and establishes a course of action for self and/or others to accomplish a specific goal.

Excellent Leadership Skills	90 to 100
Good Leadership Skills	80 to 90
Acceptable Leadership Skills	70 to 80
Poor Leadership Skills	60 to 70

Interpersonal Sensitivity

Interacts with others to bring about desired attitudes; promotes cooperative relationships; is receptive to the suggestions of others; takes actions which indicates a consideration for the feelings and needs of others; shows an awareness of the impact that one's own behavior has on others.

Excellent Interpersonal Skills	90 to 100
Good Interpersonal Skills	80 to 90
Acceptable Interpersonal Skills	70 to 80
Poor Interpersonal Skills	60 to 70

Cultural Diversity

Understands other cultures and cultural values and is confident in working with others of different and diverse backgrounds. Can identify with the feelings, thoughts, and behaviors of individuals from different cultural backgrounds.

(A high score in this area indicates that you are extremely capable of functioning in a culturally diverse workforce.)

Excellent Culture Diversity Skills	90 to 100
Good Culture Diversity Skills	80 to 90
Acceptable Culture Diversity Skills	70 to 80
Poor Culture Diversity Skills	60 to 70

Oral Communication

Orally conveys ideas or directives accurately, clearly, and to the point; speaks smoothly and fluently, positively and enthusiastically; uses gestures, posture, and eye contact with enhanced oral expression; is convincing and easy to understand; listens well to what others have to say.

Excellent Oral Communication Skills   90 to 100

Good Oral Communication Skills   80 to 90

Acceptable Oral Communication Skills 70 to 80

Poor Communication Skills   60 to 70

Problem Solving and Reasoning

The ability to solve problems and make decisions is beneficial to the fire service because high-level problem solving and reasoning saves firefighters from death and injury on a daily basis.

Problem solving is critical to the success of a firefighter because no two calls will be the same. Even similar emergency calls cannot be approached in the exact same manner. For example, two vehicle extractions could require entirely different extraction techniques and equipment. When answering your questions, it is important to demonstrate your capability to address a variety of problems and explain how your reasoning leads to a successful solution.

Ability to remember details and recall facts, identify problems, recognize signs or symptoms of a larger or broader problem, plan an appropriate plan of action to reach an objective, develop alternative solutions and evaluate their relative value and make sound decisions on the spot.

Excellent Reasoning/Problem Solving Skills   90 to 100

Good Reasoning/Problem Solving Skills   80 to 90

Acceptable Reasoning/Problem Solving Skills 70 to 80

Poor Reasoning/Problem Solving Skills   60 to 70

D: TopScore Top5 Scorecard

As mentioned above, the TopScore Top5 Scorecard will help you evaluate your use of the TopScore Top5. Your Mock Interview board should use it to the best of their ability, and you should use it during your review of the recording. The Scorecard is simple. Did you use all aspects of the Top5? How many of each did you use?

At the top of the Scoresheet, you'll be asked to score your body language, speech, and eye contact on a scale of 1-10. When considering the scale think of the following questions for each category:

Body Language
1. Did you face the board?
2. Did you have good posture?
3. Did you smile?

Speech
1. Did you use fillers such as "um" or "like"?
2. Were you clear?
3. Did you ramble?
4. Were you confident?

Eye Contact
1. Did you make eye contact with each board member?
2. Did your eye contact start with the member that asked the question?

Before you start your mock interview, you should explain the form and the TopScore process to your mock interview board. The more information they have the more accurately they will be able to score you.

Give your interviewers the TopScore Top5 Scorecard (download an easy-to-print version at www.interview911.com) and a list of potential questions. Ask them to randomly select seven questions and write each question in the provided space on the Scorecard. Additionally, ask them to track the number of Personal History, Personal Stories, Keywords, and Department Knowledge points you include in each question by marking 1-5 on the Scorecard.

Finally, request they note the following: total time of the interview, length of each answer, your body language, fidgeting and "ums," eye contact, and clarity of speech. They will rate you on a 1 to 10 scale, with 10 being the top score.

TopScore Top5 Mock Interview Scorecard

Question:
_____
_____?

Date_____

Body Language_____ Speech (ums, clarity)_____ Eye Contact_____

(Rate 1-10, 10 being the best)

Time_____

Was the question answered?	Yes	No	
Personal History	Yes	No	1 2 3 4 5
Personal Story	Yes	No	1 2 3 4 5
Department Knowledge	Yes	No	1 2 3 4 5
Keywords	Yes	No	1 2 3 4 5

NOTES

_____
_____
_____
_____

Chapter 10 Review
Putting it into Play

Consider the following to review the content presented in Chapter 10.

1) Identify a person(s) in your life to conduct a Mock Interview with you and complete the following sequence:
   1. Have them select questions and conduct the interview while recording the interview.
   2. The interviewer should use the Scoresheet and Scorecard to rate your performance.
   3. Discuss their feedback and encourage constructive criticism
   4. Watch the video of your interview so you can score your own performance.
2) Repeat and Practice!

Chapter 11
Preparation Timeline

In this chapter you'll learn:
- A. Preparation timeline
- B. Congratulations!

Rules: This chapter includes 10 Rules to help you successfully apply topics A-B listed above.

A: Preparation Timeline

Maybe you've been dreaming of being a firefighter your whole life. You know you'll get an interview someday so you're preparing now. If so, great! We wish more people would prepare with that perspective. However, most likely you have an interview in sight already. You may have a few months or a few days. You'll need to make a timeline to fit your particular situation that prioritizes your preparation. Schedule out time every day, even if some days have more availability than others.

When creating your preparation timeline keep in mind the five phases of preparation:

1. Education about the interview process: Read this book thoroughly and entirely as soon as possible.
2. Research the department and city: Finish the bulk of this as soon as possible and continue to review throughout your preparation.
3. Groundwork assignments throughout the book: Allow yourself time to complete these assignments effectively. Don't rush this step. Come back to it several days in a row.
4. Organization: The more time you can allot to this area—ideally one week—the easier your practice will be. You can interweave your organization and practice together.

5. Practice: Spend most of your time here! It may revel areas where you need to go back and spend more time refining.

Include the following benchmarks in your timeline:

Task	Complete by:
Finish the Firefighter Interview Rule Book	_____
Research the department	_____
Research the city	_____
Station visit	_____
Finish groundwork assignments throughout the book	_____
Organize answers to common questions	_____
Practice common questions using the TopScore Top5 (this should be a continual process)	_____
First casual interview with friend or family	_____
Ride-along with department	_____
Second casual interview with friend or family	_____
First Mock Interview	_____
Second Mock Interview	_____
Third casual interview with friend or family	_____
Dial in closing statements	_____
Third Mock Interview	_____

The following rules will serve as a guide on the day of your interview and after your interview:

Rule: No excessive coffee the day of the interview.

You will be nervous enough during the interview. There is no need to make it worse by consuming excessive caffeine.

Rule: 2 minutes prior, power pose!

Use your TopScore Top5 confidence and enthusiasm. **You've Got This!**

Rule: After the interview, capture important details.

One of the fastest methods for capturing as much as you can recall about the interview is to utilize the voice recorder on your cell phone immediately after the interview. Later, you can listen to it, so you can elaborate more in detail. At the very least, have a pen and paper to write down the information you remember from your interview.

Rule: Immediately after your interview, document the following:

- Names of members serving on the interview board.
- All the questions you were asked.
- Your response to the questions.
- TopScore Top5 utilization.
- What did you learn? From the board? About the process? About yourself?
- What should you have done differently?
- Send thank you cards.

Rule: Be passionate and stay committed.

Take every opportunity to learn the things that can kill you and those who can keep you safe. Share everything you learn with your brother and sister firefighters. There are many great websites and blogs that share fire training methods to help you learn. Thousands have been injured and/or killed in this great profession; please do not let those injuries and deaths go without bettering you and your crew. If this is a commitment you are not willing to make, please find another profession. We want our students to be leaders in the fire service for years to come. It's up to you whether your hiring will affect the fire service positively or negatively!

B: Congratulations!

You are now one step closer to achieving your goal.

Now comes the hard part.

Practice.

After committing to this system, we had a student come back and tell us that after his interview, one of the board members looked to the others and said, "Does anyone else feel like standing up and clapping?" This is the response you are going for!

If you'd like to take your interview to the next level, your next step is interview coaching. With interview coaching, a TopScore coach will ensure you are implementing this system correctly, and you will also have the opportunity to listen to other Mock Interviews that received a perfect score, ask questions about the process, and much more.

Visit www.interview911.com to learn more.

Good luck!

About the Authors

Mike Zolin and Rob Christensen have over 40 years of combined experience working in the fire service. They've offered interview coaching for over 15 years and have been extremely successful in helping candidates attain the job of their dreams.

"Even after coaching hundreds of candidates, I'm still amazed to see the amount of transformation with just two hours of quality coaching. Aside from being a firefighter at my dream department, helping candidates get hired is one of the best feelings in the world!" - Mike Zolin

"My favorite part about coaching is the phone calls I get after a candidate gets the job offer. I'm dedicated to leaving the fire service better than when I started, and one of the best ways I can do that is by helping the next generation of firefighters secure the job they've always dreamed of." - Rob Christensen

Learn more about interview coaching at www.interview911.com

Made in the USA
San Bernardino, CA
25 March 2019